F. D. MAURICE AND THE
CONFLICTS OF MODERN THEOLOGY

F. D. MAURICE
AND THE
CONFLICTS OF MODERN THEOLOGY

BY

ARTHUR MICHAEL RAMSEY, B.D.

*Regius Professor of Divinity in the
University of Cambridge*

THE MAURICE LECTURES, 1948

CAMBRIDGE

AT THE UNIVERSITY PRESS

1951

CAMBRIDGE
UNIVERSITY PRESS

University Printing House, Cambridge CB2 8BS, United Kingdom

Published in the United States of America by Cambridge University Press, New York

Cambridge University Press is part of the University of Cambridge.

It furthers the University's mission by disseminating knowledge in the pursuit of
education, learning and research at the highest international levels of excellence.

www.cambridge.org
Information on this title: www.cambridge.org/9781107668911

© Cambridge University Press 1951

First published 1951
First paperback edition 2014

A catalogue record for this publication is available from the British Library

ISBN 978-1-107-66891-1 Paperback

CONTENTS

Preface   *Page* 7

CHAPTER I   The Man and the Theologian   9

      II   The Kingdom of Christ   26

     III   Socialism and Eternal Life   43

    IV   Atonement and Sacrifice   58

     V   Maurice and Mansel   72

   VI   The Holy Scriptures   82

  VII   Maurice then and now   98

Bibliography   115

Index   117

PREFACE

This book includes the substance and to some extent the text of the Maurice memorial lectures given in King's College, London, in the Lent term of 1948. The lectures corresponded with the second, third and sixth chapters, and they contained also some portions of the first and seventh chapters. The rest of the book has been added since the lectures were delivered.

Though the literature about Maurice is growing, I dare to hope that the distinctive aim of this volume may give it a place within that literature. I have not attempted to provide a systematic account of Maurice's teaching, such as has been given by Dr Vidler in his admirable Hale lectures, but to trace the theological conflicts which Maurice faced and to relate them to the chief theological tendencies of the last one hundred and fifty years. In particular I do not think that any previous attempt has been made to evaluate Maurice's teaching on Atonement and Sacrifice as a whole, or to examine his methods of Biblical exegesis in relation to the subsequent trends of Biblical study. On no two subjects did Maurice more signally anticipate some of the theological work of the present day, and speak in a way which comes home to us with relevance and force.

In the study of Maurice's character and personality I have found particular help in two sketches of him by contemporaries: the one is by Julia Wedgwood in her *Nineteenth Century Teachers*, and the other is by R. H. Hutton in his *Modern Guides of English Thought in Matters of Faith*, and together they form a valuable supplement to the Biography beloved by every student of Maurice. In the study of the theological movements of the last century there is no lack of older works which share rather naïvely in one or other of the enthusiasms of the time, and of more recent works which are coloured by the violent reaction from everything 'liberal'. By far the most successful attempt to see the whole period in perspective was made, I think, by Dr J. M. Creed in his Hulsean lectures on *The Divinity of Jesus Christ*, and my debt to him is great.

I have to thank the Rev. R. E. Cant, Vice-Principal of St Chad's College, Durham for reading my manuscript and giving me the benefit of his acute historical and theological judgment. And I cannot end without thanking once more the Council of King's College for honouring me with the Maurice lectureship. To lecture on Maurice, within the walls of the College and in the centenary year of the movement of 1848, was to me an unforgettable privilege.

MICHAEL RAMSEY

DURHAM, 1949

THE MAN AND THE THEOLOGIAN

On October 27, 1853, the Council of King's College, London, passed a resolution that they 'feel it to be their painful duty to declare that the continuance of Professor Maurice's connection with the College as one of its Professors would be seriously detrimental to its usefulness'. A few years hence the College will be keeping the centenary of that momentous day in its history; and though a hundred years is long enough · as a space for repentance, it may prove too short a time for a *final* assessment of one of the greatest figures in the history of Christianity in our land. 'The fathers have eaten sour grapes, and the children's teeth are set on edge.' None the less a *fresh* assessment is in process, and no greater honour could fall to me than to be allowed, by the kindness of the Council and Professorial Board, to make in this place my own very small contribution towards this.

Though Maurice was a theologian to the core, he belongs to the story of English 'Life and Letters' in a way that is remarkable for one whose writings were nearly all published sermons and whose literary style was sometimes execrable. He has a place not only in ecclesiastical history but in the circle of such men as Carlyle, Mill, Tennyson, Leslie Stephen. Carlyle thought him worthy of more than one pungent paragraph; Mill reckoned with him as a mind of the highest calibre; Tennyson greeted his expulsion from your College by a poem to him, and Leslie Stephen's markedly unsympathetic sketch in the *Dictionary of National Biography* is an inverted tribute to his influence. And though Maurice never met Coleridge he did more than any other man to carry the message of Coleridge into the England of the middle years of the century. We cannot separate Maurice the theologian from Maurice the man; and though these lectures will be about the theology, we shall pause sometimes for a glimpse of the man amongst his contemporaries.

I

Born at Lowestoft in 1805, Frederick Denison Maurice came of a Unitarian household: perhaps 'household' is hardly correct, for while the father, a minister, clung to the end to this creed the mother and four children deserted it for other forms of faith. It was a family saddened by religious divisions; but Frederick to the end regarded the Trinitarian creed, which he came to embrace passionately, not as an abandonment of the doctrine of unity which he had learnt from his father but as an unfolding of its true meaning. 'I not only believe in the Trinity in Unity', he was to write, 'but I find in it the centre of all my beliefs: the rest of my spirit when I contemplate myself or mankind. But, strange as it may seem, I owe the depth of this belief in great measure to my training in my home. The very name that was used to describe the denial of this doctrine is the one which expresses to me the end that I have been compelled even in spite of myself to seek.'[1] I have time only to recall his boyhood at Frenchay near Bristol; his years at Trinity, where Julius Hare was his teacher, Plato the biggest influence amongst his studies, and Sterling his closest friend; his migration to Trinity Hall on account of its special facilities for the study of law; his agonizing problem of conscience which caused him to leave Cambridge without a degree, for he could not yet declare himself a member of the Church of England; his few years in London writing for the *Westminster Review* and editing the *Athenaeum* in collaboration with Sterling; his conviction that he had come to believe as the Church of England believes and that ordination was his calling; his return to University life—this time at Exeter College, Oxford; his baptism; his graduation; his defence of the obligation to sign the XXXIX Articles on matriculation. This defence was elaborated a few years later in *Subscription No Bondage*, his first theological tract: 'Subscription is a declaration of the terms on which the University professes to teach its pupils; upon what terms they agree to learn; it is fairer to express those terms than to conceal them, and they are not an unfit introduction to a general education in humanity and physics—because they are theological and on that account very valuable, and the Articles may contribute to the reconciliation of what is positive in all Christian sects.'

Carry the story just one stage further. Maurice was

---

[1] *The Life of Frederick Denison Maurice* (1885), I, p. 41.

ordained deacon in 1834, and after two years in Warwickshire as a country curate he is back in London, chaplain of Guy's Hospital. Two more years, and he has written his first theological book, and perhaps the greatest of them all, *The Kingdom of Christ*. His characteristic ideas are already formed, and are finding mature and powerful expression. To say that the *whole* of Maurice, theologian-philosopher-man, was in this book would be an exaggeration: yet it would not be a grotesque exaggeration. Thirty-six years old, Maurice had found his message and spoken it.

Affectionate in his nature, Maurice is seen at every stage of his life as one of a circle. There was first his family. His closeness to his parents was unbroken, and nothing is more touching than the letter to his father at the time of his ordination, explaining something of his changed outlook and declaring his debt to his home. At Cambridge there was the Apostles' club: Sterling, Trench, Hallam were next to Maurice its most vigorous minds. Sterling was always held in special affection. He took orders, and was for a very short time Hare's curate at Hurstmonceaux; but he abandoned this calling as a mistake and, under Carlyle's influence, moved steadily farther from the faith of the Church. Maurice married Sterling's sister-in-law, Annie Barton, in 1837. Sterling's death in 1844 and Annie's death a year later were shattering blows: he ever reproached himself for what he felt to be his failure to lead Sterling in the way of faith. In 1849 he married Georgiana, the half-sister of Julius Hare, who had himself married Maurice's sister four years earlier.

It was no clericalist circle, for near to it were two of the greatest lay figures of the century, Carlyle in Chelsea and Coleridge in Highgate. Carlyle was intimate with Sterling, and aroused Maurice's resentment for drawing Sterling away from Coleridge and the Christian faith. Carlyle in a kindlier mood could write 'Maurice has come twice athwart me: a man I like always for his delicacy, his ingenuity and earnestness: he is wonderfully patient of me, I often think; and I ought to esteem his way of thought at its full worth, and let it *live* in me, if I could. Hitherto, I regret to confess, it is mainly moonshine and *Spitzfindigkeit*, and will not live. But the man is good, and does live in me'.[1] But, when exasperated, he wrote, 'One of the most entirely uninteresting men of genius that I can meet with in society is poor Maurice to me. All twisted, screwed, wire-drawn, with such a restless sensitiveness: the utmost inability to let nature have fair play with him'.[2] Maurice on his part, fresh from attending a lecture by Carlyle, laments that by missing the meaning of the Incarnation that great man lived in a 'world without a centre', and indulged in 'silly rant about the great bosom of nature'; but his vagaries were corrected by a 'real abhorrence of what is base and false' so that 'his inconsistencies . . . seem to me the greatest providential blessings, explaining wherein he is false and enabling us to receive his truth'.[3]

On the other side of London there was Coleridge.

---

[1] *New letters of Thomas Carlyle*, ed. Alexander Carlyle, I, p. 29.
[2] *Ibid.* I, p. 108-9.
[3] *Life of F.D.M.*, I, p. 282-3.

Now a sick and ageing man, weakened by years of the opium habit, Coleridge drew many of the young intellectuals of the day by his amazing conversation. Though Sterling was at his feet, Maurice never met him. But if it is true that apart from Coleridge we cannot understand the history of theology in the nineteenth century, it is as true that apart from him we cannot see Maurice in his right perspective.

II

The importance of Coleridge becomes apparent if we ask what reading could be recommended to a layman in the eighteen-thirties who was looking for some vindication of the reasonableness of Christian belief and found the older method of 'evidences' for an external and authoritative revelation no longer satisfying. 'Evidences of Christianity!' said Coleridge. 'I am weary of the word. Make a man feel the want of it; rouse him if you can to the self-knowledge of his need of it; and you may safely trust it to its own evidence'. Coleridge threw aside the apologetic which dwelt upon nature as the perfect machine which must have God as its designer, and led people to think instead about those aspects of man which cannot be classified with nature: his will, and 'reason', and sense of sin. The Christian faith is shewn to be congruous with the truth about man himself, and the Christian Church to be congruous with man's social being. It meant much that Coleridge 'could still, after Hume and Voltaire had done their best and worst with him, profess himself an orthodox Christian, and say and point to the

Church of England, with its singular old rubrics and surplices at Allhallowtide, *Esto perpetua*'.[1]

But Coleridge did far more than stand in a gap. He justified Mill's description of him as one of the seminal minds of the century by introducing a new *method* into the discussion of Christian theology. May we remind ourselves of the main lines of his thought, as it is found especially in his *Aids to Reflection* and in his posthumously published *Confessions of an Inquiring Spirit*? He recognizes the real, causal activity of the will, inexplicable from the life of nature: he sees the will as the principle of our personality. He recognizes the existence of moral evil whereby man is 'a fallen creature', and knows it—not just because he is told so in the narratives of Genesis, but because he is 'diseased in that will, which is the true and only significance of the word I, or the intelligent self', He insists upon the distinction between our Reason and our Understanding: the Understanding signifies the use of rational processes in the narrower sense, the Reason includes sense and imagination as well as understanding and is equivalent to 'a total act of the soul'. He claims that by Reason, in this inclusive sense, men may hold real communion with God Himself, and their capacity for seeing

[1] Carlyle *Life of John Sterling*, p. 62. The whole chapter, entitled 'Coleridge', is one of Carlyle's very best. For Coleridge's theology see Hort in *Cambridge Essays* (1856), J. Tulloch in his *Movements of Religious Thought in Great Britain during the Nineteenth Century* (1893), and V. F. Storr in his *Development of English Theology in the Nineteenth Century* (a good chapter in a book which is in the main unsatisfactory, not least in its treatment of Maurice). C. R. Sanders in his *Coleridge and the Broad Church Movement* (1942) is invaluable in the mass of material which he collects, but his treatment of the relation of Maurice to Coleridge hardly does justice to the distinctive place of Maurice as a theologian.

the light is itself the presence of the light shining in their whole being. He thus commends Christianity not simply as a revelation *ab extra* through Book or Church, but as the crown and perfection of all intelligence, the truth in which all lesser truths find their fulfilment. As for the Bible, Coleridge discourages a fear of critical movements: read the Bible like any other book—and you will find that it is *not* like any other: 'whatever *finds* me, bears witness for itself that it has proceeded from a Holy Spirit'. Coleridge is not discarding the unique revelation in the Biblical history: he claims to be shewing how that revelation vindicates itself as revelation in the conscience and mind of man. Similarly he is not discarding dogma: he claims to be approaching it through its practical bearing upon man's need and its self-authentication through its congruity with the truth of man's being.

It is a far cry from teaching of this sort to our present-day post-liberal dogmatic and Biblical theology. But I would beg anyone whom this description of Coleridge rouses to impatience to read Dr J. M. Creed's Hulsean lectures, *The Divinity of Jesus Christ*, where an awareness of the many weaknesses of the nineteenth century is not allowed to oust a shrewd appreciation of what such men as Schleiermacher on the continent and Coleridge in England were doing. The notion of 'Revelation *in vacuo*' had gone with the turn of the century: the concept of Revelation needed vindication in new ways, on the lines of the congruity of its truth with what man knows (and even feels!) about himself and about nature. Of course the risk of a shallow immanentism lurked round the corner: but, says Dr Creed, 'Christus consummator is the description of our Lord which answers most adequately to the type of doctrine which we have been consider-ing. Men such as Schleiermacher, Coleridge, F. D. Maurice, Westcott, cannot and will not deny the working of God's spirit wherever it may be traced, but they did not cease to affirm their faith in Christ as one who completes what is truly but imperfectly present elsewhere . . . We can no longer think in their terms. But their doctrine is, as I judge, to this extent still valid: first, if our treatment of the manifold data of religions, past and present, is to be fruitful, we need some general conception of religion to help us, before we can proceed to value and to classify. And in the second place the Romantics were right when they insisted that actual religion is always positive and specific'.[1] Dr Creed uses the word 'Romantic' to cover a big variety of writers, but if Coleridge belongs to them in broad description, he was nearer than many of them to the main Christian tradition. He was indeed engaged in expounding the nature of 'religion', but he so did it as to be the defender not only of the Biblical revelation but also of the Church—and the Church of England.

The conception of the Church was an essential part of Coleridge's thought. In his *On the Constitution of Church and State according to the Idea of Each* he parted with the conception of Church and State as two aspects of the same community and expounded the

[1] *The Divinity of Jesus Christ*, pp. 39, 40.

idea of a national Church which is not identical with
the nation since it is a portion of the Church Catholic
and Apostolic. Coleridge in a sense prefigured the
Oxford Movement: 'My fixed principle is: that a
Christianity without a Church exercising spiritual
authority is vanity and delusion. And my belief is,
that when Popery is rushing in on us like an inundation,
the nation will find it to be so'.[1] But it is not among
the Tractarians that his real successors were to be
found. One whose judgment was seldom at fault,
R. W. Church, wrote in his notebook at the time
when he was reading for a fellowship, 'There is something in Maurice, and his master Coleridge, which
wakens thought in me more than any other writings
almost: with all their imputed mysticism they seem to
me to say plain things as often as most people'.[2] *His master
Coleridge*: it is a strong phrase, and to understand
Maurice we must consider both its truth and its limits.

At Trinity Maurice had 'defended Coleridge's meta-
physics and Wordsworth's poetry against the Utilitarian
teaching'. More still, 'I had no inclination to infidelity.
Coleridge had done much to preserve me from that'.[3]
Perhaps it was on account of his shyness and diffidence
that he never went to Highgate to see Coleridge. Yet
all the while Coleridge had been providing, not perhaps the doctrines about which Maurice thought, so

[1] *Aids to Reflection*, p. 295. Newman says that though Coleridge 'indulged
a liberty of speculation which no Christian can tolerate, and advocated
conclusions which were often heathen rather than Christian', yet he 'made
trial of his age . . . and succeeded in interesting its genius in the cause of
Catholic truth'. (*Essays Critical and Historical*, I, p. 268.)

[2] *Life and letters of Dean Church*, p. 17.

[3] *Life of F.D.M.*, I, p. 177.

much as some of the methods by which he thought. Characteristic ideas of the one man reappear in the other. That theology is concerned with God Himself and not with systems of thought about Him; that theology is not *in vacuo* but the consummation of all other studies; that divine truth is accessible to every man and not only to those capable of certain experiences, and is apprehended by the whole man and not by some spiritual faculty alone; that the Reason is more inclusive than the Understanding; that 'evidences' are ineffectual without God Himself at work in the soul; that there is a Catholic and Apostolic Church beyond all parties and systems; that parties are an abomination—these are themes about which the language of both men is sometimes similar, and an expert student of their writings might make mistakes in assigning quotations to the right author. Common to both of them also is a peculiar mixture of the conservative and the radical: a devotion to the old institutions combined with a wish to overthrow the more familiar grounds of defending them. Both of them, finally, disliked Carlyle's idea of heroes ('Nothing is so ignominious as the craving for great men to appear, as if the universe depended onthem'.—Maurice, *The Friendship of Books*, p. 293), for in both of them was the knowledge of man's essential frailty. Coleridge knew that the will is diseased, Maurice that the heart is deceitful and desperately sick.

Maurice, however, was guarded in his expressions of his debt to Coleridge, and the fullest of these expressions—the 'Dedication' prefaced to the second edition of *The Kingdom of Christ*—is in part an apology for a divergence of which Maurice was already beginning to be conscious. When all is said, Maurice was something which Coleridge was not. Of itself the theology of Coleridge, like that of other of the 'Romantics' of Dr Creed's comprehensive nomenclature, could lead on to some of the characteristic weaknesses of the age of liberalism. The doctrine of universal communion with God *can* issue in a doctrine of 'diffused incarnation', with no room for the particularity of the Gospel; and the explanation of Biblical authority in terms of 'whatever finds me' *can* issue in a dissolution of the authority which it seeks to commend. The point about Maurice is that for him these aberrations were not remotely conceivable. While his thinking was partly done in forms which he had learnt from Coleridge, he stood as a theologian *within* the Bible in a way that Coleridge never did; and, while he went as far as it is possible to go in recognizing the light that lighteth every man, his soul rested in the unique *act* of the Incarnation. The two criticisms which he made of Coleridge are significant. One is that Coleridge used a 'jargon of abstract terms where plain words would be preferable'[1]; the other is that Coleridge attended to ideas at the expense of historical facts.[2] These criticisms hint at the difference between the two men. If Coleridge was a philosopher intent upon showing how the truth about man pointed to the Biblical revelation as its crown, Maurice was a theologian who

---

[1] *Life of F.D.M.*, II, p. 168.
[2] Ibid., I p. 251.

could, from within the Bible, expound that revelation in the Bible's own terms and categories.

III

The convictions about theology which meant most to Maurice were formed in his mind early, and they find expression again and again in his letters and books.

There is first the reality of God, as distinct from human notions and theories about God. 'The one thought which possesses me most at this time, and I may say has always possessed me, is that we have been dosing our people with religion when what they want is not this but the Living God, and that we are threatened now, not with the loss of religious feeling so-called or of religious notions, but with Atheism.'[1] On all sides he saw devout men substituting for faith in God sometimes a system of church dogma, sometimes a belief in an experience of conversion or justification, sometimes an interest in an affair called religion: the last of these being the preoccupation of the Broad Church School, which had 'succumbed to that which seems to me the greatest disease of our time, that we talk about God and our religion, and do not confess Him as a living God'.[2] Maurice recovered for the word 'Theology' its strict and proper meaning.

Then there is the truth that God is creator. The world was made through the eternal Son; and in the Incarnation He comes not as an alien invader into an unknown foreign land, but as man's own maker into

---

[1] *Life of F.D.M.*, I, p. 369.
[2] Ibid., II, p. 359.

human lives of which He is already the indwelling principle. 'The truth is that every man is in Christ; the condemnation of every man is that he will not own the truth; he will not act as if this were true, he will not believe that which is the truth, that, except he were joined to Christ, he could not think, breathe, live a single hour. This is the monstrous lie which the devil palms upon poor sinners: "You are something apart from Christ. You have a separate, independent existence".'[1] Often Maurice uses the phrase 'Christ is in every man'. The words have puzzled many. They do not imply that Maurice denies sin and the Fall, but that he will not allow the Fall to be the basis of theology.[2] God made man in his own image, the image which is perfectly known in Christ. And the life in Christ, while it is brought to us as the utterly new gift of a Redeemer, is none the less the life of our true and original selves as men.

It was alleged by some of Maurice's contemporary critics, including the ablest of them, J. H. Rigg, the Methodist theologian, that his doctrine of creation was Neoplatonist rather than Biblical and that he was influenced by an emanationist view which identified all

[1] *Life of F.D.M.* I, p. 155.

[2] It is here especially that Maurice had been influenced by Thomas Erskine of Linlathen, the lawyer turned theologian, who repudiated the current teaching in the Kirk on the predestination of a large portion of the human race to damnation. Erskine's influence on Maurice began before he went up to Cambridge (*Life of F.D.M.*, I, p. 43), and deepened when Maurice read *The Brazen Serpent* as an undergraduate (ibid. p. 108). He visited Erskine in 1847 (ibid. p. 443), and dedicated to him his *Prophets and Kings of the Old Testament*. Their friendship grew, and they frequently corresponded until Erskine's death in 1870.

reality with the mind of the divine Logos and blurred the distinction between creator and creature.[1] It is indeed a moot question how far Platonism affected Maurice's basic assumptions; but those who made this particular criticism of him were apt to lose sight of the extent to which the Alexandrine tradition can appeal to Pauline and Johannine teaching for its conception of creation as summed up in the Son of God.

Maurice avowed the Bible and Plato to be the twin sources of his thinking. Plato had come alive to him through the lectures of Hare at Cambridge; he wrote to Hort in 1850: 'I have never taken up any dialogue of Plato without getting more from it than from any book not in the Bible'. Inevitably his Platonism coloured his Biblical exegesis; and it led him to a tendency to expound the whole Bible through the spectacles of his own interpretation of the Johannine prologue. But I hope to show in a later lecture that it was the Bible which really dominated; and in it Maurice saw 'the history of a divine descent into the misery to wrestle with it, to bring back the victims of it into the home of peace from which they had wandered'.[2]

Thirdly, Maurice saw himself not as initiating new developments in theology but as unearthing aspects of

[1] Cf. J. H. Rigg, *Modern Anglican Theology* (third edition, 1880) Ch. VIII. Rigg supports his contention by quoting such passages as these. 'I look upon Christ's death and resurrection as revelations of the Son of God, in whom all things had stood from the first, in whom God had looked upon His creature man from the first.'—*Unity of the New Testament*, p. 367'. The Eternal Word is affirmed to be that form or type in whom the Divine Artist fashioned the whole universe.'—*Epistles of St John*, p. 131.

[2] *The Gospel of the Kingdom of Heaven*, p. 158.

the orthodox faith which contemporary systems and expositions hid from sight. To his abhorrence of all 'isms' he linked a devotion to the formularies of the faith. The Creeds, the Prayer Book, the Articles have never had a warmer adherent. 'I look upon them (the Articles) as an invaluable charter, protecting us against a system which once enslaved us and might enslave us again; protecting us also against the systems of the present day—against 'Records' and 'Times' news-papers, and Bishops of Exeter and Heads of Houses. Without the Articles we should be at the mercy of one or other of these, or be trampled upon by all in suc-cession'.[1] Maurice wrote not as a defender of the faith —for the faith was, for him, always its own commen-dation, but as one who would uncover the faith which its defenders so often bury.

Men thought of Maurice as a heretic; but I would end this lecture with some words of one who would have liked Maurice to be a heretic and lamented that he was not. John Stuart Mill wrote thus: 'I have so deep a respect for Maurice's character and purposes as well as for his great mental gifts that it is with some un-willingness I say anything which may seem to place him on a less high eminence than I would gladly be able to accord to him. But I have always thought that there was more intellectual power wasted in Maurice than in any other of my contemporaries. Few of them certainly had so much to waste. Great powers of generalization, rare ingenuity and subtlety, and a wide perception of important and obvious truths, served

[1] *Life of F.D.M.*, I, p. 399.

him not for putting something better into the place of the worthless heap of received opinions on the great subjects of thought, but for proving to his own mind that the Church of England had known everything from the first, and that all the truths on the ground of which the Church and orthodoxy had been attacked (many of which he saw as clearly as anyone) are not only consistent with the Thirty-Nine Articles, but are better understood and expressed in these Articles than by anyone who rejects them'.[1]

Mill's words do Maurice some injustice, but they throw some light upon why it was that he exasperated so many within the Church and helped so many on or beyond its frontiers. His devotion to the historic faith of the Church was linked with a reverence for the instinct for truth which led many to reject some of its contemporary parodies.

[1] J. S. Mill, *Autobiography*, p. 153.

CHAPTER II

THE KINGDOM OF CHRIST

I

By *Subscription No Bondage* Maurice had given pleasure to
the Tractarians, and for a short while they thought of
him hopefully as one who would take their part. At
the end of 1836 he was, with their support though
without any mutual consultation, nominated as a can-
didate for the Chair of Political Economy at Oxford;
but within a few months they had withdrawn their
support and he had withdrawn his candidature. The
rupture is dramatically described by Maurice himself.
He walked across Clapham Common reading Pusey's
Tract on Baptism; and, as he read, it came home to him
that there was a gulf between them. How near Maurice
stood to the Tractarian belief in the Church as a divine
society is fairly stated by Julia Wedgwood: 'If we were
forced to give him a party name, we should find it least
misleading to call him a High Churchman'.[1] How big
the gulf came to appear is shown by Pusey's remark,
many years later, that he and Maurice worshipped
different Gods.

Though the rupture occurred over the doctrine of
Baptism, its deeper cause was a difference of theological method. Both the Tractarians and Maurice
believed in a divine society with divinely ordered

[1] *Nineteenth Century Teachers*, p. 45.

marks of its Catholic and Apostolic character. The Tractarians dwelt upon it as a supernatural system standing over against heretical forms of Christianity and contemporary movements without. Maurice was at pains to show how it is related to the half-truths and broken lights of both, and offers the reality of which they were parodies and distorted witnesses.

The Kingdom of Christ; or Hints on the Principles, Ordinances, and Constitution of the Catholic Church, in letters to a Member of the Society of Friends appeared in 1838. It had already been issued in the previous year as *Letters to a Member of the Society of Friends* in twelve parts. A Second Edition, considerably revised and including the dedication to the Rev. Derwent Coleridge, came in 1842. It was thus contemporaneous with the early crisis of the Oxford Movement; and like the Tracts it expounded a theology definite and dogmatic, based upon Scripture and Tradition. But Maurice does what no dogmatic theologian of his time succeeded in doing, and what few dogmatic theologians of any time have done—he meets other people on their own ground. Thus he examines in turn the positive convictions of a Quaker, an orthodox Protestant, a Unitarian, a contemporary philosopher; he draws out with sympathy the positive principle of each; he acknowledges whatever validity that positive principle possesses; and he goes on to show how in each case the positive principle fails to maintain itself as a result of being twisted into a self-contained system. Finally he turns from the partial theological systems with their divisive tendencies, and he asks what are the signs of a 'spiritual and universal Kingdom' which goes behind these systems. The signs are Baptism, the Creed, Forms of Worship, the Eucharist, the Episcopate, the Scriptures: here are the marks of the society, founded by God, wherein God may deliver us from the bondage of man-made schemes of religion.

The first half of the book is a sort of Socratic converse with those whose positions he analyses and criticizes. *O si sic omnes!* With the din of the controversies of the 1830s so near, Maurice sets himself not just to expound truth as he sees it, but to know and to understand his Quaker, his Protestant, his Unitarian. He can describe what the inner light means to a Quaker, what it is that the Unitarian is really saying when he demands a moral simplicity whose absence he fears in contemporary dogmatic Christianity, what justification by faith means to a Lutheran.[1] But to this patient understanding Maurice adds a vigorous exposure of fallacies. The Quaker, he shows, distorts his own positive principle of the inner light, by failing to see how the event of the Incarnation is its clue, and in consequence his spirituality becomes secularized and

[1] Maurice (like Julius Hare) is one of the few exceptions to the almost constant failure of Anglican theologians to understand Luther. 'His [*sc.* Luther's] assertion of the right and duty to believe in God who justifies was the great blow, the deadly blow, to those who make faith consist in assent to propositions ... When Luther, and still more Melancthon, succumbed to propositions in their later days, when assent to the doctrine of justification was substituted for belief in the Justifier, Protestantism went into the lean, sickly and yet contentious stage of its existence.' *Life of F.D.M.*, II, p. 615. Maurice's criticisms of Lutheranism are penetrating, but I have more than once heard tributes to Maurice from Lutheran theologians abroad who regard him as the Anglican who understood what Luther meant.

corrupted. The Protestant, because he treats his principle of justification by faith as a shibboleth, slips from faith in Christ the justifier into belief in an experience of being justified: and great is the fall. The Unitarian is concerned to maintain at all costs the simplicity of the divine love, but shies at the central fact, God of God, light of light, very God of very God, which vindicates his own principle. It is systems which are everywhere at fault, the systems made by the orthodox no less than those made by heretics; and Maurice turns several times in the book to the errors of Rome. Two especially receive his attention: Rome's tendency to regard the sacramental system as a mechanism whereby men strive to win contact with an absent Christ, as if to climb up to heaven to bring Christ down, instead of proclaiming Christ to be nigh already to men in their hearts; and Rome's tendency to substitute belief in a structure of reasoning for faith in Christ Himself. But Maurice regarded the latter tendency not as a peculiarity of Western Scholasticism, but as the recurring temptation of all whose business it is to reason about their faith.

He now turns to construction. Is there in existence a divine society? We find such a society described in Scripture. Israel is the Church of God—first a family, then a nation, wherein king, priest and prophet, temple, law and sacrifice are elements in one inseparable unity. It was not at the time common to expound the Church as the Israel of God, and to seek its meaning within Scripture as a whole; and no other exponent of the doctrine of the Church in Maurice's day—

Newman, Palmer, Arnold, Gladstone—succeeded in treating the Church in a manner so thoroughly scriptural. Maurice sees in scripture the principles of the Church which now is, because there still exists the holy nation, the people of God; and of this Catholic Church Baptism, Creed, Liturgy, Episcopate, Scripture are the signs. In each case Maurice emphasizes not views about the fact, but the fact itself in its witness to the existence of a universal Church. His treatment of Baptism is difficult, and I will say a word about it presently; and his treatment of Scripture will claim a lecture to itself. The *Creeds* 'are the defence of the scriptures and the poor man against the attempt of doctors to confuse the one and to rob the other'. The *Eucharist* is both sacrifice and sacrament, setting forth Christ in His present self-offering to the Father and enabling us to participate in His self-offering. Maurice shrinks from language about a presence 'in' or 'under' the elements, for in the Eucharist we are lifted up to heaven where Christ is and must not regard the rite as a means to drag Christ down. (He was constantly wont to emphasize the Ascension in his Eucharistic teaching.)[1]

As for the *Ministry*, our Lord appointed the twelve not only to be His representatives but to share His own ministry as an ever-present prophet, king and priest. Though the institution of the ministry is a major theme of the Gospel narratives it was the Resurrection which gave to the ministry of the twelve its

[1] Apart from *The Kingdom of Christ* Maurice's Eucharistic teaching is to be found specially in *Sermons on the Prayer Book* and in *Sermons, First Series*, Vol. I, Ch. I-V. Cf. *Life of F.D.M.*, II, p. 365.

intrinsic character by interweaving it with Christ's own perpetual ministry, risen from the dead and active through them. From this foundation Maurice draws big conclusions. 'Were those', he asks, 'who succeeded to the apostolic office to reckon that they derived their powers less immediately from Christ than those who received their commission from Him when He was with them on earth?' Further, 'those nations who have preserved the episcopal institution have a right to believe that they have preserved one of the appointed and indispensable signs of a spiritual and universal society'. Maurice sees in the episcopate not an archaism or a party cry, but the sign of the existence on earth of a Catholic Church greater than schools of thought or theological systems or sectional types of Christian experience. Does office puff up, and lead to arrogance? Maurice knows that bishops and priests can be proud and tyrannical. But the remedy, he tells us, is not to lower our doctrine of the office, but to appeal from the misuse of the office to the fact of the office itself as a rebuke to those who misuse it. 'Abolish our ordination', he exclaims, 'and you lose the strongest testimony which you have against our sins.'

From the Catholic Church and its signs Maurice turns specifically to his own land. The principle of catholicity, so far from disallowing national churches, vindicates their necessity. While the existence of the Catholic Church witnesses against the evils of nationalism in religion, the existence of national churches benefits the Catholic Church by hindering it from becoming a worldly despotism. To a church, however, the word 'Protestant' ought never to be applied: 'Protestant' is a proper description for a nation, but only 'Catholic' for a church.

Is there in England a Catholic Church with its recognizable marks? There is, and the 'signs of the constitution' attest its presence. But within it are those who contend for systems, and create parties in their defence. The Liberal, the Evangelical, the Catholic are each of them stirred by the sight of some urgent spiritual need of the time and strive to meet it by the truth which each of them cherishes. But the result is disastrous. The Liberal desires to commend the faith to the thought of the age, and his method is to dilute the formularies: but 'what if the abandonment either of the Prayers or the Articles, or the reduction of them to our present standards of thought, should bring the Church into the most flat and hopeless monotony, should so level her to the superstitions of the *nineteenth* century, so divorce her from the past and the future, that all expansion would for ever be impossible?' The Evangelical laments that outward religion has usurped the place of vital faith, and strives to recover the latter. But in his efforts to do this he denies the status of the baptized, and makes a particular conversion experience the basis of the life in Christ; he denies the reality of the Eucharistic gift, and tells men that it is 'only a picture or likeness, which, by a violent act of our will, we may turn into a reality'.[1] The Catholic laments the lack of belief in

[1] Cf. *Life of F.D.M.*, I, p. 139: 'are there not some persons who preach Faith instead of preaching Christ?'.

the visible Church and its discipline, and his attempts to inculcate it involve him in some strange paradoxes. He often speaks as if catholicity meant holding correct opinions, and was not inherent in the fact of our baptism; as if it were a treasure to be won by discipline, and not a treasure already given. Thus 'congregations are treated as if they had never obtained their baptismal rights'; splendid assurances about the powers of the Church are combined with 'the most strange uncertainty about the terms under which she exists'; and the denouncers of 'private judgment' are found to be its regular practisers! In no case does the partisan *desire* the thing which results: 'My charge against each is that he defeats his own object.'

So Maurice passes on to his celebrated denunciation of parties. The Church is defined by the acts of God which create and sustain it, systems are defined by the opinions held by their upholders: the difference is a radical one. But there can be something even worse than parties—the attitude of those who in their cocksureness at being 'non-party' are naïvely inventing a new non-party type of their own: 'Since a school which should be formed to oppose all schools must of necessity be more mischievous than any of them; and a school which pretended to amalgamate the doctrines of all other schools would be, I think, more mischievous than that,[1]

---

[1] Cf. Maurice's words on eclecticism, in a letter to Daniel Macmillan, 'Oh, there is nothing so emasculating as the atmosphere of Eclecticism! Who that has dwelt in it has not longed for the keen mountain misty air of Calvinism, for anything, however biting, that would stir him to action?' *Life of F.D.M.*, I, p. 339. Cf. ibid. II, p. 138, 'those who said "we are of Christ" were the worst canters and dividers of all'!

I do pray earnestly that if any such schools should arise, they may come to nought; and that, if what I have written in this book should tend even in the least degree to favour the establishment of them, it may come to nought'.

II

Maurice was, like the Tractarians, contending for the dogma of the Holy Catholic Church; but his methods and his emphasis were different from theirs. They viewed the Church as the home of the redeemed, full of grace and truth, in contrast with a sinful age where grace was repudiated and truth denied. He viewed the Church not only as the home of the redeemed, but as the sign that God had redeemed the whole human race and that the whole human race was potentially in Christ. This led him to combine an insistence upon the definite character of the signs of the Church's constitution with an unwillingness to define the Church's present boundaries. Asked about the limits of the Church he answers, 'I cannot answer the question; I believe only One can answer it; I am content to leave it with Him.'[1] Again, because he connected the doctrine of the Church with the doctrine of Creation he looked upon the characteristic movements of thought of the age not simply as enemies to be fought in the Tractarian manner, but as half-lights to be cleansed and fulfilled. To the conception of *Christus Consummator* he added that of *Ecclesia Consummatrix*.

In the light of all this the very difficult controversy

[1] *The Epistle to the Hebrews*, p. cxxiv.

between Maurice and Pusey over Baptism becomes a little more intelligible. To Pusey the context of Baptism was the sinful world on the one hand and the Church as the ark of salvation on the other: in Baptism we are brought from the sinful world into the Church, we are given a new nature by regeneration and we receive the infusion of the Holy Spirit. To Maurice the context was a world not ruled by the evil one but already redeemed by Christ: every child that is born is born into a world already redeemed, and in Baptism this truth is proclaimed and the child is put into relation to it. Pusey seemed to Maurice, no doubt unjustly, to postulate a change in the divine favour elicited by Baptism. Maurice seemed to Pusey to deny that anything *happened* in Baptism, and to reduce it to a public affirmation that the child was already a son of God. It is certain that Maurice believed that much happened in Baptism, but he subordinated this to what had already happened in the redemption of mankind by the Son of God. It was far from easy for him to reconcile his teaching with the Prayer Book phrase 'my baptism, wherein I was *made* a member of Christ, the child of God and an inheritor of the Kingdom of Heaven', and his attempt to do so involved some straining of language.[1] Throughout Maurice's theology there ran the principle *Werde was Du bist*: become what you are. In redemption we become what we are as men made in God's image: in baptism we become what we are as members of a redeemed human race: in confirmation we have not a completion of baptism but an acceptance

[1] Cf. a letter to Kingsley, *Life of F.D.M.* II, pp. 221-5.

of its completeness. It cannot be denied that this principle is Biblical, and that western theology has been too inclined to overlook it: but it seems to some good judges that to press the principle as far as Maurice did is to miss the Biblical emphasis upon those *momenta* in history in which salvation is offered and accepted.

It was the Tractarians who, concentrating upon the single principle of 'our Apostolic Descent', recovered the doctrine of the Holy Catholic Church, and they did so only through conflict. The conflict involved the party feeling which Maurice greatly deplored: the Tractarians, he said, 'are under the influence of the destructive spirit of the age, at times endeavouring to pull down other men's truth because it is not the same portion as their own'.[1] It involved also what Maurice felt to be the note of archaism in their teaching. 'Their error, I think, consists in opposing to the spirit of this present age, the spirit of a former age, instead of the ever-living and active Spirit of God, of which the spirit of each age is at once the adversary and the parody'.[2] Maurice saw much which they did not see, and he foreshadowed theological developments which were to come. He saw the possibility of relating the doctrine of the Church to the doctrine of mankind as recapitulated in the Second Adam. He saw the possibility of applying the sacramental principle to the common life no less than to the institutional Church. Hence *The Kingdom of Christ* is a prophetic work. Its

[1] *Life of F.D.M.*, I, p. 205.
[2] Ibid. I, p. 226.

36

method foreshadows the social sacramentalism of Stewart Headlam and Scott Holland, the cosmic conception of the Church taught today by French Roman Catholic theologians and the more Biblical presentation of the Church as the Israel of God which has become familiar since H. F. Hamilton's *The People of God*. Neither Maurice nor Maurice's great book could have produced the Catholic revival in the Church of England; but he, while that revival was only a few years old, unconsciously interpreted its wider significance, gave warning of its coming perils and hinted at some of its final fruits.

The contrast between the Tractarian and the Maurician doctrines of the Church is in part the contrast between the Latin and the Alexandrine outlook. But the roots of the contrast are within the Bible. There the Church is a society, with an historical origin and a boundary, standing over against the world; there also the Church is inherent in the creation of mankind, and definable as the whole race of mankind redeemed. These diverse aspects of the Church have sometimes become doctrines defined in mutual antagonism; but a sound theology demands the validity of both in union and tension.

III

Professor Tulloch says that Maurice 'could find no life for his soul in the Evangelical or in the Anglican tradition. It was not the theology of either but theology itself that he was contending for'.[1] These words are nearly, but not quite, true. Certainly 'theology

[1] *Movements of Religious Thought in Britain during the 19th Century*, p. 291.

itself' was Maurice's first and last absorption. But the life of Maurice shows him happy to find 'theology itself' mediated through a loving loyalty to the Church of England.

It was as a theologian in the strict sense that Maurice abhorred parties in the Church—as well as journalism of every kind. He was convinced that the process of organizing people in defence of particular sets of Church principles results in distorting the proportion of the faith, in admitting a spirit of propaganda which is very different from a zeal for truth, in substituting a Pelagian idea of unity in our possession of certain opinions for the right idea of unity in our common reception of the gifts of God.

The ministry of Maurice was one of immense activity as preacher, pastor, priest. It was nearly all spent in London. The chaplaincy of Guy's Hospital brought him into touch with men, women and children of the poorest classes, and set his mind at work upon a legion of social questions. In 1840 he added to these labours the chair of English Literature at King's College; and in 1846, when its school of theology began, he became Professor of Ecclesiastical History and at the same time exchanged his work at Guy's for the chaplaincy of Lincoln's Inn. It was there that the greater number of his published sermons were delivered, beginning with the Boyle lectures, which formed one of the more lucid and popular of his books, *The Religions of the World*. And besides the academic duties and the preaching there was always some other activity. Now it was the class for working men, with the volume,

The Epistles of St John, as its legacy. Now it was the presidency of the Queen's College designed for the education of governesses—the first serious essay in the higher education of women. A little later there was the headship of the Working Men's College in Russell Square. If he preached too much, and published too many sermons so that the volumes are sometimes repetitive,[1] the message never seems stale: for he loved his fellow men, and walked humbly with his God.

Maurice was an Anglican, devoted to the Prayer Book and eager to expound its contents to his flock. To the Prayer Book he had a devotion second only to his reverence for the Bible. 'I hope', he says, 'you will never hear from me such phrases as "our incomparable liturgy": I do not think we are to praise the liturgy but to use it. When we do not want it for our life, we may begin to talk of it as a beautiful composition. Thanks be to God, it does not remind us of its own merits when it is bidding us draw near to Him.' His view of worship is intensely corporate: this is how he explains the use of the Psalter. 'By acts of worship we come to understand how that which is David's becomes ours in Him who is the son of David and the son of God. The service brings before us on the same day Psalms written in the most different states of mind, expressive of the most different feelings. If we have sympathized in one it often seems a painful effort to join in the rest.

---

[1] My own 'short list' would be *Sermons on the Prayer Book, Patriarchs and Lawgivers of the Old Testament, The Gospel of St John*, and *The Doctrine of Sacrifice*.

And so it must, as long as we look upon prayers and praises as expression of our moods, as long as we are not joining in them because we belong to a family and count it our highest glory to lose ourselves in it and in Him who is the head of it'. These quotations are from *Sermons on the Prayer Book*, a volume which, together with *The Lord's Prayer* and *The Church a Family* (addresses on the occasional offices), gives Maurice's practical teaching on worship. He kept scrupulously the fasts and festivals of the Church. He drew daily worshippers to the chapel of Lincoln's Inn by his reverent conduct of the office. His was a ministry in which preaching and liturgy were close together and interpreted each other.

Maurice was a penitent. The sorrows which he had to bear were for him, as for Pusey, occasions of self-scrutiny and confession of sin. The death of his wife left him 'much more oppressed with the sense of sin than of sorrow. I cry to be forgiven for the eight years in which one of the truest and noblest of God's children was trusted to one who could not help or guide her aright, rather than to be comforted in the desolation which is appointed to me'.[1] 'All my thoughts of Sterling are mingled with shame and self-reproach, which it is better to lay before God, who does understand it, than before the public or even friends who would not'. His severity to himself for his own failings was sometimes a cause of his violent attacks upon others. When he denounced rigidity, harshness, clerical narrowness his victims did not commonly

[1] *Life of F.D.M.*, I, p. 405.

realize that he felt deeply the same faults in himself, and that the war without was at one with a war within. Acutely conscious of the solidarity of the human race, he felt the sins of the age and confessed them; and he confessed his own failure to feel them more.

In the character of Maurice there was an unusual blending of gentleness and violence. His unfailing store of sympathy and tenderness towards men and women made him the more intense in his antagonism to 'systems'. Similarly both clarity and mistiness appear in his teaching and writing. He grasped certain principles plainly, and repeated them constantly. But his exposition of them was too often enclosed within pages of denunciation of the way in which other people expounded them; and it was and is often puzzling to distinguish what he was plucking down and what he was setting up. Hence it sometimes happened that people who had a real desire to understand Maurice found him exasperating. Julia Wedgwood refers to his trick of turning an awkward corner in an argument by a reference to a 'bedridden woman, who was always being introduced to us as the infallible arbiter of spiritual problems perplexing to the minds of scholars and profound thinkers, generally in order to rebuke the pride of our intellect, but nearly as often that she might reflect upon our spiritual exclusiveness'.[1] J. B. Mozley complained that Maurice 'appears to regard established forms of belief as things to be knocked down . . . but after knocking down the established formula, when he comes to give us his own, we find

[1] *Nineteenth Century Teachers*, p. 40.

that it does not, substantially, so much differ from the established one'.[1] What chiefly moved Maurice to violence was his conviction that the truth of God was near to men and women in its self-authenticating force, if only we would be content to say what the truth is and not to confuse it with 'systems', which are less orthodox than they sound, or with the business of 'religion', which puts ourselves instead of God in the centre.[2]

Maurice's point was an extraordinarily difficult one for his contemporaries to grasp. As Hare said, 'When it pleases God to send a prophet into the world, on his brow there is written "I came not to bring peace but a sword".'

[1] *Essays Historical and Theological*, II, p. 228.

[2] 'It is a very great and serious question indeed, whether our patronage of "Christianity" is not subverting the revelation of Christ.' *What is Revelation?*, p. 105.

CHAPTER III

SOCIALISM AND ETERNAL LIFE

A HUNDRED years ago the constitution of King's College left it largely in the hands of a body of subscribers. 'The majority', says Maurice's biographer, 'consisted of wealthy peers of sufficiently strong religious and ecclesiastical feeling to have contributed largely to an institution intended to support the Church of England against dissent. It was tolerably certain therefore that such a body would pretty faithfully represent the current opinion of the wealthy classes—namely the opinion of which *The Record* would be in part the expression and in part the travesty'. This was one of the reasons why Dr Jelf, the very conscientious Principal, found Maurice so big a handful. A press campaign against Maurice was raging, comparable in its stupid and discreditable malice with that which raged against Lord Haldane in the early years of the 1914 war. Outside the College many made no attempt to be fair or to understand: within the College Dr Jelf tried very hard to be fair and failed to understand. There was the growing complaint about Maurice's 'Socialism' and over this a breach was just avoided. There was the charge of heresy about Eternal Punishment, in connection with the volume *Theological Essays*, and over this the crash came. It is not only chronology which suggests the grouping of the two subjects of this lecture together: there was an underlying unity in Maurice's doctrines about 'Life', here in industrial England—and in eternity.

I

First, there was 'Socialism'. 'My dear Maurice', the Principal writes in November 1851, 'I see nothing in any writing avowedly your own inconsistent with your position as professor of divinity in this College . . . I wish I could speak in similar terms of Mr Kingsley's writings, but I confess I have rarely met with a more reckless and dangerous writer. It is to be hoped that you will openly disavow Mr Kingsley. Otherwise it may be said justly ''Mr Maurice is identified with Mr Kingsley, and Mr Kingsley is identified with Mr Holyoake, and Mr Holyoake is identified with Tom Paine . . .''. Thus there are only three links between King's College and the author of *The Rights of Man*.' Maurice made a powerful reply: so far from encouraging atheism and revolution his 'socialist' activities had not ineffectively combated both. A committee of inquiry exonerated him, but some words in its Report about the misfortune of Maurice's name being mixed up with the writers of certain publications shewed that there was no understanding, and no peace.

Mr Reckitt's recent Scott Holland lectures have dealt with this aspect of Maurice's teaching with such learning and illumination that it would be impertinent for me to wander in his tracks. But Maurice is all of a piece. We cannot cut him into two and call one half theology and the other socialism. The Co-operative

Societies and the Working Men's College sprang from the same theological root as the *Sermons on the Prayer Book*.

It is in one of these sermons, in Advent 1848 amid the alarms of revolutions abroad and Chartism at home, that Maurice asked the congregation in Lincoln's Inn: 'Do you think that the invasion of Palestine by Sennacherib is a greater event than the overthrow of nearly all the greatest powers in Christendom?' That sentence is a clue. While the Tractarians saw in the revolutionary forces of the time something to be kept at bay by the building of a wall of supernatural doctrine and other-worldly anti-rationalism, Maurice saw in those forces a set of aspirations to be met by churchmen upon their own level and, if not to be corrected and purged, at least to be spoken to with some appreciation of what they were 'at'. This was essentially the method which Maurice had employed in *The Kingdom of Christ*, in the stricter field of theology. Just as he met Quaker, Protestant, Unitarian on their own ground, trying to fulfil all righteousness and to employ the principle of *Christus Consummator*, so now he does the same, in a different context, with violent men with empty stomachs and crude ideas about the ways of improving their lot.

Hence Maurice's 'Socialism'. It had nothing to do with collectivism, with the nationalization of transport or the levelling of incomes. It meant in practice two things. First, it meant commending the Christian faith to people by knowing and understanding their aspirations. In doing this, Maurice was too good a theologian to treat the Gospel as a panacea, or to detach some portion of it and call it the 'social' Gospel. The Gospel remains the Gospel, with its correlative demand of brotherly conduct between man and man. Secondly, it meant inducing work-people to look after one another and themselves in a Christian way. 'Competition is put forth as the law of the universe. That is a lie. The time is coming for us to declare that it is a lie. I see no way but by association for work instead of for striking. Hence my notion of a Tailors' Association.' Both these convictions led Maurice straight into immense labour, for 'the devil will not in the least mind my saying the Church has a bearing upon all common life, if I take no pains that my particular Church should bear upon it at all'. The immense labour, with Kingsley, Ludlow, Hughes and others as his associates, included the Tracts entitled *Politics for the People*, the Tailors' Co-operative Societies, and the Working Men's College in Red Lion Square. The story has been fully told by Dr Raven in his book *Christian Socialism 1848-1854*. I am here attempting no more than a reminder of it.

But why call it 'Socialism'? It seems that there were two motives behind Maurice's use of the word. In part the word was simply a provocative challenge on two fronts. 'Christian Socialism is the only title which will define our object, and will commit us at once to the conflict we must engage in sooner or later with the *Unsocial Christians* and the *Unchristian Socialists*.' In part the word could express a theology, and Maurice was attempting to rescue it for theology. His belief in God

the blessed Trinity led on to the belief that throughout
the world which God the blessed Trinity created there
is imbedded a law, a divine order, not to be con-
structed by mankind or awaited as the climax of historical progress, but rather to be dug out, perceived,
and lived out at every point where it is perceived.
As Maurice was one of those theologians whose doctrine of the Trinity includes a principle of subordination among the Persons of the Triune God, so he
affirms a principle of subordination in the law of
brotherhood upon earth. Politically this law involved
not egalitarianism, still less democracy (which
Maurice never liked), but theocracy expressed through
a monarchy with divine right; and that small portion
of Maurice's theory which could be expressed politically resembled faintly a sort of Toryism. But
Maurice was not concerned to sketch a vision of a
Christian realm, or to plan a Christian political pro-
gramme: he is too apocalyptic in his thinking to paint
pictures of a day when 'earth shall be fair and all her
peoples one'. He sought rather to discover the
Christian foundation of man's life in society; to say
what this foundation is; and *to do certain things
without delay* when his perception of the foundation
demanded them. Do the will, and learn more of the
doctrine.

Such is 'Socialism'. 'My dear Ludlow', Maurice
writes fifteen years later, 'I have never repented of
having been united with you in maintaining that
co-operation as applied to trade has a Christian foundation. And the phrase, "Christian Socialism", I still

think was a desirable defiance of two kinds of popular prejudice, and worth all the obloquy and ridicule which it incurred.'[1] The movement of 1847-8 was a day of very small things, but of a great theology which demanded that those small things should happen.

II

Within the same chapter of Maurice's biography as the Christian Socialist Movement there is recorded the controversy about Eternal Life. Waves and storms were raging against Maurice.

In 1853 he published *Theological Essays*. In my humble judgment it is one of the weakest of Maurice's books. It is the work of a man on edge; and throughout it the proportions of theological exposition are distorted by a preoccupation with those points where Maurice was irritated by contemporary theologians. Many good things are in the book, but we can sympathize with Dean Church, who complained of its 'tormenting indistinctness'. While several passages received severe criticism it was a passage near the end of the book which caused the explosion, since Maurice in these pages seemed to be denying the possibility of everlasting loss for the impenitent. The Council met on 27 October, 1853. A motion was brought forward, condemning the book as 'calculated to unsettle the minds of the theological students of King's College': an amendment to refer the complaint to a Committee of theologians was—in spite of Mr Gladstone's support—lost, and the original motion

[1] *Life of F.D.M.*, II, 550.

was carried.[1] All was done courteously and kindly: but it was an act of expulsion, not a voluntary resignation.

Though the *casus belli* was drawn from the concluding pages of *Theological Essays*, the clearest statement of the point at issue may be found in the correspondence between Maurice and Hort in the second chapter of the second volume of the *Life*. To contemporary Christian thought the alternatives at the day of judgment were everlasting reward and everlasting punishment: the words 'everlasting' and 'eternal' were taken as identical: eternity meant endless duration. We have Hort's testimony that few Cambridge teachers of the day were able to distinguish 'eternal' and 'everlasting'. Now Maurice was not a universalist: he was unable to endorse the familiar Broad Churchman's position: 'God is loving and therefore all must be saved: hell is incredible.' To Maurice loss was a real possibility to be meditated upon. But his thought upon life and death was cast in exclusively Johannine terms, and indeed in a thorough-going Platonist interpretation of those terms. His central conviction was: 'This is life eternal, to know Thee the one true God'. 'I cannot', he said, 'apply the idea of time to the word eternal. I must see eternity as something altogether out of time, and connect it with Him who was and is to come.' On the one side there is life eternal: timeless, qualitative, possible here and now, the life of union with God.

[1] Notice should be taken of the honourable part played by Bishop Samuel Wilberforce, who wrote to Maurice to make sure that he understood his teaching correctly, and then strove his utmost to prevent the condemnation: cf. *Life of Bishop Wilberforce*, II, pp. 208-18.

On the other side there is the separation from God which is sin, the state which is itself the state of death. Sin is itself death, loss, the loneliness of self-centred isolation. But concerning this state of loss, while it may be the fate of souls which persist in impenitence, we cannot call it everlasting, for ideas of duration are out of place and are an importation of temporal categories into a realm where we do not know that they apply. Further, when a soul is gripped in the death of sin the love of God strives to win it, and we dare not say that this divine striving ceases on account of the accident of bodily death: 'that God's love should pursue the sinner in this world, and would cease to open any vista of fatherly welcome to him when an accident or an illness dissolved his connection with the body, was what Maurice disbelieved with all his soul'.[1]

In sum, Maurice denied that those who die impenitent are certainly lost, that loss can rightly have the adjective 'everlasting' fixed to it, that the fire which Scripture and the Athanasian Creed calls 'aeternus' or *aionios* is rightly taken to have temporal duration. That loss may happen, he will not deny. Indeed he leaves the matter very nearly where Dean Church was to leave it in his great sermon in *Human Life and its Conditions*. 'I dare not pronounce', says Maurice, 'what are the possibilities of resistance in a human will to the loving will of God. There are times when they seem to me (thinking of myself more than others) almost infinite. But I know there is something which

[1] Julia Wedgwood, *Nineteenth Century Teachers*, p. 43.

must be infinite in an abyss of love beyond the abyss of death. More than that I cannot know, but God knows —I leave myself and all to him.'[1]

The category of 'eternal life' which Maurice was employing was unintelligible to most of his contemporaries. They had a clear-cut picture of a human race divided at death into everlasting heaven and everlasting hell. Maurice was in a different universe of discourse. It was assumed that he was a universalist: no hell, then moral laxity; and the Council dismissed him because the *morals* of its students were imperilled. *Maxima debetur puero reverentia*, and the students then were younger than they are now.

But besides the spate of vituperative literature there was the critical analysis of Maurice's position made by one of the finest minds of Anglican divinity in the century: J. B. Mozley. It is printed in the second volume of his *Essays Historical and Theological*. Mozley begins with some gentle criticism of Maurice as a writer, 'It is fortunate for the world', he says, 'that all the men who come forward to instruct and enlighten it are not cast in the same mould, and that some, according to their bent, reason and others prophesy. There is a depth of mind which explains itself and unfolds its ideas in regular order, and there is also a depth which asserts itself, which throws out its contents, to produce their impression and make their way as such. The former is the more perfect method humanly, the latter is more divine. It is a kind of inspiration, and has an authoritativeness from an

[1] *Theological Essays*, p. 406.

51

absence of art. Indeed, in proportion as minds are full of an idea or ideas, it is difficult for them to arrange or methodize them, or put them in the order of proof as addressed to other intelligences . . . It may be pretty safely said that no one can see clearly except he stands still. But the act of standing still is exceedingly distasteful to minds under the impulse of peculiar ideas . . . Mr Maurice will, we are sure, not take it amiss if we put him in the order of prophets, and assign force of conviction rather than of argument as his forte.'[1] This is a memorable paragraph. There are those who put Mozley first amongst the theologians of the time, just as there are those who put Maurice first. And here the one is being frank about the other. Men seem to be born with the one sort of mind or the other.

Mozley's criticisms were shrewd. First, Maurice holds that eternity means 'pure existence', 'a vital truth, so that Mr Maurice could not live for a day without it, and will maintain the urgent cause of preaching it to peasants and labourers, to ploughboys and artisans'. But the conception, Mozley points out, is a very difficult one, a trained philosopher finds it very hard to grasp. And our Lord was addressing not philosophers but simple people when He gave his stern warnings about future reward and punishment. Must we not think that these warnings really meant what our Lord's hearers would take them to mean? 'These shall go into everlasting life, and the wicked into everlasting fire.' Maurice's appeal to Scripture,

[1] *Essays Historical and Theological*, II, pp. 256-7.

and his plea for the plain man, are being turned against himself! Secondly, Maurice identifies eternity with life in union with God, a state of qualitative perfection. But, says Mozley, this is half a conception. Aquinas, following Augustine, defines eternity as *interminabilis atque tota simul et perfecta possessio vitae*. Why dwell on the *tota simul et perfecta*, and ignore the *interminabilis?* Maurice is building on a defective foundation in philosophy. Lastly, Mozley seems on strong ground in saying that Maurice's plea that his view is that of the formularies is a special plea: is it not more natural to interpret the formularies after the mind of the age in which they were compiled? Maurice no doubt would answer that the purpose of formularies is to protect us from the mind of particular ages by witnessing to a revealed truth of timeless significance!

It was a clash between two types of eschatological thinking which have long been present within the Christian Church. There is the Hebraic type, with its conception of a series of events in temporal sequence, a conception which the Latin mind was ready to adopt and to arrange in logical precision. There is the Johannine-Platonist type, with its conceptions of life with God and of death apart from Him, and of the goal not as time prolonged but as the escape from time into eternity. The Maurice controversy shows how far the latter idea could be completely submerged and lost sight of in western theological thought: indeed one recalls the voice of Bishop Gore saying: 'Von Hügel is a dear old thing, but I dont understand all this talk about a *totum simul*.'

In its turn Maurice's eschatology, like other parts of his theology, has a too exclusively Johannine-Platonist character. Today we may be on the way towards an eschatology in which the Hebraic and the Hellenic elements are held in unity, albeit in tension. But if we are on the way towards such a synthesis, we have to remember that the mere recognition of the Johannine conception was recovered in English theological thought only by blood and tears.[1]

III

Socialism and eternal life may seem far removed one from another, belonging to different worlds and hardly suitable for a single lecture. To Maurice they were both expressions of one and the same theology, the theology of the Divine Unity which he had learnt in his father's house and had relearnt as the Trinity in Unity of his baptism. Socialism meant the recognition of the love of the Triune God expressed in the order of creation and in the law of brotherhood derived from that order. Eternal life meant that life in union with the Father and the Son, a life whose centre is not self but the Holy Spirit.

In a letter to Kingsley, Maurice shows how belief in the Triune God was the root, and even the essence, of his Christian socialism. 'The Name into which we were baptized, the Name which was to bind together all

[1] The view that 'eternal' denotes a non-temporal existence is defended by F. H. Brabant in his Bampton lectures, *Time and Eternity in Christian Thought*. But it is repudiated by Edwyn Bevan in his Gifford lectures, *Symbolism and Religion*, and recently by O. Cullmann in *Christus und die Zeit*.

nations, comes but to me more and more as that which must at last break these fetters. I can find none of my liberal friends to whom that language does not sound utterly wild and incomprehensible, while the orthodox would give me for the eternal Name the dry dogma of the Trinity—an opinion which I may brag of as *mine*, given me by I know not what councils of noisy doctors and to be retained in spite of the reason, which it is said to contradict—lest I should be cast into hell for rejecting it. I am sure that this Name is the infinite all-embracing charity which I may proclaim to publicans and harlots as that in which they are living and moving and having their being, in which they may believe, and by which they may be raised to the freedom and righteousness and fellowship for which they were created.'[1] Since the Triune God is the creator of the human race, the likeness of His eternal charity dwells in the human race, and the Trinity in Unity is the source of human fellowship in those who repent of their self-centred isolation and discover the true principle of their being.[2]

So too with eternal loss. Its essence is not the

---

[1] *Life of F.D.M.*, II, p. 494.

[2] It has been recently noted by Professor D. M. Baillie that there is in Anglican theologians a tendency to 'sharpen the distinction between the Persons of the Trinity, and to go farther than theology has been accustomed to go in the direction of regarding them as distinct personal beings between whom there can be a social relationship.' (*God was in Christ*, p. 137). Dr. Baillie traces this tendency largely to the Gifford lectures of Dr C. C. J. Webb and shows its connection with the social message of a number of theologians. But the tendency is far older than Webb, and Maurice illustrates it signally. It would, however, be unjust to say that the tendency in Maurice's case ever approached *Tritheism*: the lessons of his home were too strong for that.

rejection of an intellectual formula, but the spurning of the divine charity of which the formula speaks. 'If I took the Athanasian Creed to mean that anyone who does not hold certain intellectual notions about the Trinity must without doubt perish everlastingly, I must take it to condemn not Unitarians, not Arians, not Tritheists of every kind merely, but all women, children, poor people, whose minds have not been exercised in logical inquiries, and are not capable of understanding logical results . . . But what other sense will the words bear? . . . The name of the Trinity, the Father, the Son and the Holy Ghost is, as the fathers and schoolmen said continually, the name of the Infinite Charity, the perfect love, the full vision of which is that beatific vision for which saints and angels long even while they dwell in it. To lose this, to be separated from this, to be cut off from the Name in which we live and move and have our being, is everlasting death . . . But who incur this separation? I know not. You and I, while we are repeating the Creed, may be incurring it.'[1]

Maurice long maintained that *his* interpretation of the *Quicunque vult* was the natural one. In 1864 he desires to continue the public use of that Creed, 'Because I believe the Creed asserts some great principles which are not asserted so clearly elsewhere', and 'because I count it an advantage to be able to explain to my congregation why I do not consider the true and simple meaning of the words, that meaning which is given them by the popular opinion of our

[1] *Life of F.D.M.*, II, pp. 412-3.

day'.[1] But in 1867 the realization that it 'does not express the belief or conviction of most of those who use it' weighs with him: only 'I wish that before it is given up, people would make themselves masters of some of its more common and least disputed expressions'.[2] And in 1870, 'it is pretty sure to be banished from our service now, and I wish that it should'.[3] The prevalence of an erroneous interpretation of it had, in Maurice's view, made its popular recitation unreal. As with the Thirty-Nine Articles, so with the *Quicunque*, Maurice came to realize that he had been claiming too much.

Nothing, however, could shake Maurice's hold upon the faith of the Blessed Trinity, as the key to socialism, to eternal life, to the unity of the human race, and to the secret of man's being.

[1] *Life of F.D.M.*, II, p. 480.
[2] Ibid., II, p. 564.
[3] Ibid., II, p. 618.

CHAPTER IV

ATONEMENT AND SACRIFICE

I

MAURICE's treatment of the Atonement in *Theological Essays* exposed him to violent attacks, though it was not, like his teaching on Eternal Punishment, the occasion of a heresy trial. Nowhere did his contemporaries misjudge him more than in his doctrine of the Cross; and nowhere, in my own belief, was his constructive achievement as a theologian higher. He saw beyond the ruts into which the treatment of the doctrine had fallen, and anticipated a synthesis which has only in very recent years come into sight. And I am not aware that any attempt has been made to describe and assess his teaching on this subject as a whole. It is insufficient to judge him by reference to the brief chapter in *Theological Essays* alone: his work on *The Doctrine of Sacrifice* and many incidental passages in other works have to be taken into account.[1]

[1] It is remarkable that standard works on the history of the doctrine of Atonement, such as J. K. Mozley's, give no account of Maurice's teaching. Dr Grensted in his *History of the Doctrine of the Atonement* mentions only *Theological Essays* and so gives an incomplete picture of Maurice's doctrine. Dr Headlam, in his Maurice lectures entitled *The Atonement*, makes the opposite mistake of concentrating exclusively upon *The Doctrine of Sacrifice*. There is a more judicious account in Scott Lidgett's *The Spiritual Principle of the Atonement*, and a reference to the importance of Maurice's teaching in the preface by A. G. Hebert to his translation of Aulen's *Christus Victor*.

It was in connection with the chapter on the Atonement in *Theological Essays* that J. B. Mozley made the criticism of Maurice, quoted elsewhere in these lectures,[1] to the effect that he made it his business to attack the accepted form of a doctrine but, when called upon to give his own version, would provide something not unlike the formula which he had attacked. In the presentations of the Atonement which were most common at the time Maurice could find much to rouse him. The orthodoxy on the subject was usually identified with a doctrine of penal substitution: by His death our Lord bore the penalty which was our due, so that the penalty need not fall upon ourselves. In the cruder presentations of this doctrine the Son was regarded as appeasing an estranged Father. In the more balanced presentations it was not forgotten that the Atonement has its root in the Father's loving initiative; but it was not uncommon to isolate the Cross, to dwell upon Christ as man's substitute and to forget Christ as man's representative, and to leave the relation between Christ's death and its manward effects unexplained. Recoiling from an unsatisfactory treatment of the Cross which offended their consciences, many Broad Churchmen tended to embrace a purely 'exemplarist' doctrine in its place.

Maurice attacks the cruder form of the current doctrine. But he goes further; and, using the familiar argument of the 'exemplarist' school—that the transference of the penalty to the Son is unjust—he denies that the death of Christ is rightly regarded as penal and

[1] See p. 41.

that the satisfaction consisted in the death. Having made this denial (*Theological Essays*, 3rd edition, p. 117), he goes on to affirm something not unlike what he denies. 'Since nowhere is the contrast between infinite Love and infinite Evil brought before us as it is there, we have the fullest right to affirm that the Cross exhibits the wrath of God against sin, and the endurance of that wrath by the well-beloved Son. For wrath against that which is unlovely is not the counter-acting force to love, but the attribute of it. Without it love would be a name, and not a reality. And the endurance of that wrath or punishment by Christ came from His acknowledging that it proceeded from love, and His willingness that it should not be quenched till it had effected its full loving purpose. The endurance of that wrath was the proof that He bore in the truest and strictest sense the sins of the world, feeling them with that anguish with which only a perfectly pure and holy Being, who is also a perfectly sympathizing and gracious Being, can feel the sins of others. Whatever diminished His purity must have diminished His sympathy. Complete suffering with sin and for sin is only possible in one who is completely free from it.'

In the paragraph just quoted Maurice expressed what he felt to be the heart of the matter. But he went on to say that it should be presented without the use of explanations which shock the conscience. And he makes six *caveats* about the presentation of it. (1) At all costs it must be emphasized that the Will of God is the ground of all that is right and true and gracious. (2)

The Son of God in heaven and on earth was one with the Father; and on earth *His whole life* was an exhibition of the Father's will, an entire submission to it. (3) Christ is the Lord of men, and 'if we speak of Christ as taking upon himself the sins of men by some artificial substitution, we deny that He is their actual representative'. (4) Christ has actually rescued men from the power of death, that is from the devil and not from God. (5) The Lamb of God taketh away the sin of the world: the sin itself and not merely the penalty of it. (6) Christ satisfied the Father by presenting 'His own holiness and love, that in His sacrifice and death all that holiness and love came forth completely'. Finally Maurice weaves these six points together into a summary of his faith: the Father's will to all good; the Son obeying that will 'by entering into the lowest condition into which men have fallen through their sin'; the Father's abiding satisfaction in the Son, a satisfaction 'to be fully drawn out by the Death of the Cross'; the death as a sacrifice, 'the only complete sacrifice ever offered': 'is not this, in the highest sense, Atonement?'

A modern reader of these pages of Maurice would be struck by the degree of adherence to tradition which they suggest. But what struck his contemporaries was his insistence upon abandoning the rigour of the penal conception, and the obscurity of some of the language: and this was attributed to a movement of Maurice's mind towards a purely 'Abelardian' doctrine. The same impression is recorded by Dr Grensted: 'This is not language easy of interpretation, and indeed it is difficult to draw out any clear theory of Atonement from Maurice's writings. But it is obvious how similar his general standpoint is to that of contemporary German and English exponents of the Moral Theory'.[1] I do not think this is a true verdict. Without doubt Maurice is developing the 'manward' aspect of the Atonement, and without doubt he is obscure. But I think that the obscurity is because Maurice's thought fails to fit the familiar classifications of Atonement theories, just because he is grasping (to borrow McLeod Campbell's famous phrase) that the Atonement must be 'seen in its own light'. Christ indeed bore our penalty—yet we cannot call His death penal, because His penalty-bearing was penetrated through and through by His gracious, loving obedience. Christ indeed made satisfaction—yet we cannot equate the satisfaction with the bare fact of the death, since the death was the expression of an obedience which made all the difference to it. Christ indeed bore instead of us what we could not ourselves bear—but it was not by a divine transference of penalty to Him from us as a *substitute*, so much as by His coming into our region which lies under the divine wrath and from the midst of it making the perfect acceptance of that wrath as our *representative*. Maurice rejected the crude expressions of the penal theory for those reasons which the 'exemplarist' school commonly adduced: yet he was not abandoning the 'objective' type of doctrine in favour of theirs. Rather was he hinting at some of those reshapings of the 'objective' doctrine which Campbell, Forsyth and others were to make; and he was seeing

[1] *History of the Doctrine of the Atonement*, p. 356.

beyond the futile conflict between Penal Substitution and Exemplarism into regions of doctrine which had been long lost sight of altogether—the classic doctrine of Christ's victory and the doctrine of Christ's sacrifice as the sacrifice of our representative and head.

II

These wider regions of doctrine are revisited in Maurice's *The Doctrine of Sacrifice*. Though it is a volume of sermons, it is, after *The Kingdom of Christ*, his most systematic work and perhaps his best. It is strangely old-fashioned, with its pre-critical and often arbitrary exegesis of patriarchal stories. Yet it is of today, with its anticipation of lessons which Aulen and others have been teaching us.

In this book Maurice keeps to Biblical exposition throughout. He begins with the stories about sacrifice in the Pentateuch: Cain and Abel, Noah, Abraham, Moses. He emphasizes the divine ordering of the sacrifices: they represent not man's attempt to extort blessings from God or to change God's will, but man's acceptance of a divine command and man's will to acknowledge himself dependent, submissive, thankful for God's gifts and eager to dedicate himself to the giver of them. Fancifully perhaps but with an eye to a distinction which runs through the history of worship, Maurice sees Cain as the man who offers in fear and anxiety, striving to get something: whereas Abel offers in submission, acknowledging his dependence upon God and not pressing the claims of his own will. 'The meaning of these two sacrifices goes through the history: the confession of dependence and trust on a righteous being, from whom life came, which made Abel's offering an acceptable one; the proud feeling of Cain that he had something to give, which led to the discontent when he received nothing in return for his gift.' Then Noah, living in a day of judgment and delivered in order that he and his might worship and serve God and so the creator's design be not totally destroyed, offers sacrifice in self-surrender to that design: 'the sacrifice assumes that eternal right is in the ruler of the universe, that all the caprice has come from man in his struggle to be an independent being . . . and, when the sense of dependence is restored to man by the discovery of his own impotence, he brings the sacrifice which is the expression of his surrender'. Then Abraham: 'the sacrifice', he cries, 'that I must offer is the very gift which has caused me all my joy, that belongs to God. I can only express my dependence, my thankfulness, by laying my son on the altar'. So 'he takes his son, he goes three days' journey to Mount Moriah, his son is with him—*but he has already offered up himself.*' The story goes on; and Maurice deals in similar fashion with the Passover, the sacrifices of the Law, and finally with David in Psalm 51. This is the climax. 'The humiliation of David, which showed him that he had nothing of his own to offer; that he must come empty-handed, broken-hearted, to receive of God that which He alone could give, a right and true spirit—this humiliation, while it seemed to undermine the legal doctrine of sacrifice, actually vindicated it, and placed it on its proper ground . . .

Sacrifice was brought out in its fullest and most radical sense, as the giving up, not of something belonging to the man, but of the man himself. Till he made that oblation, he was in a wrong state. When it was made he was in a restored state—in the state in which God had intended him to be, a dependent creature, a trusting creature, capable of receiving his Maker's image.' (p. 100).

Maurice now turns to the New Testament. He takes first the description of Christ in I Peter i. 19-20 as the 'lamb . . . who verily was fore-ordained before the foundation of the world'. The principle of sacrifice which God had been revealing to man in the Old Testament has its root in the being of God Himself. 'There is a ground of sacrifice in the divine nature; in that submission of the Son to the Father, that perfect unity of purpose, will, substance, between them, whence the obedience and fellowship of all unfallen beings, the obedience and fellowship of all restored beings, must be derived, and by which they are sustained.' (p. 109). Sacrifice is not contingent upon Sin; it is 'implied in the very original of the universe', 'it was expressed in the divine obedience of the Son before the worlds were' and 'the manifestation of it in the latter days was to take away sin, because Sin and Sacrifice are the eternal opposites' (p. 118).

The sacrifice of Christ in history was a revelation of the original principle of the world, and an act of redemption which restored that principle by breaking the power of sin. How was this done? Maurice gives an answer by expounding many passages from the

Epistles. Especially memorable is his exposition of 'Christ made Sin for us' (Ch. XII): from a description of the union of love and repulsion in Christ's dealing with the man with an unclean spirit he passes to the dereliction on Calvary as the commentary upon the words 'made sin for us'; and, repeating a distinction made in *Theological Essays*, he says, 'He knows no sin, *therefore* He identifies Himself with the sinner. That phrase, "identifies Himself with the sinner", is nearer, I think, to the sense of the epistle than the phrase "takes the consequence or the punishment of sin". But still, do you not feel how much feebler it is than his, feebler in spirit more even than in form? It conveys no impression of the sense, the taste, the anguish of sin, which St Paul would have us think of, as realized by the Son of God—a sense, a taste, an anguish which are not only compatible with the not knowing sin, but would be impossible in anyone who did know it' (p. 188).

But, above all, Maurice emphasizes the *victorious* character of Christ's sacrifice. 'God was there seen in the power and might of His love, in direct conflict with Sin and Death and Hell, triumphing over them by Sacrifice' (p. 256). Nor is this victory only a dramatic victory over personified evil forces. It is, through men's union with Christ in the power of the Spirit, a replacing of the rule of Sin within them by the rule of Sacrifice; and the heading of one of Maurice's chapters well expresses this: 'Christ's sacrifice a power to form us after His likeness'. 'He comes to make us priests; to give us all the power of offering up spiritual sacrifices to God; of offering up ourselves; of feeling with our brethren; of bearing their burdens; of entering into the holy place with them and for them: of presenting to them the image of Christ's Father and their Father' (p. 289).

Christus Consummator is the goal of Maurice's doctrine, Sacrifice is the character of God, and the true principle of man, made in God's image. Ousted by sin, this principle is vindicated by Christ's bloody sacrifice for sinners, and restored as the principle of our lives. Thus 'we see beneath all evil, beneath the universe itself, that eternal and original union of the Father and the Son which this day tells us of; that union which was never fully manifested till the Only-begotten by the eternal Spirit offered Himself to God. The revelation of that primal unity is the revelation of the ground on which all things stand. It is the revelation of an order which sustains all the intercourse and society of men. It is the revelation of that which sin has ever been seeking to destroy, and which at last has overcome sin. It is the revelation of that perfect harmony to which we look forward when all things are gathered up in Christ . . . when the law of sacrifice shall be the acknowledged law of all creation' (p. 194).

It is not difficult to find fault with Maurice's Old Testament exegesis.[1] He idealizes the sacrificial system, and interprets it in terms of a conception which is not that of Hebrew religion in its historical context. But he lays hold upon an ultimate truth—

[1] This was done, trenchantly, by J. H. Rigg, *Modern Anglican Theology*, chs. XVI and XVII.

that the godward offering which God demands of man exists in its perfection only within the being of God Himself. This view of sacrifice, as related to the being of God and the constitution of the world, was to have a particularly powerful exposition in Scott Holland's sermons on sacrifice in his *Logic and Life* (1882). But theology still awaits a comprehensive treatment of sacrifice as man's privilege and vocation in relation to Christ's sacrifice and priesthood, to the eternal glorifying of the Father by the Son and to the constitution of the created world: a treatment which does justice both to the reinterpretation of sacrifice through Christ, and to the history of sacrifice in primitive times.

The Doctrine of Sacrifice was a great book for its time. In the rejection of the usual form of the doctrine and in his emphasis upon the manward appeal of the Cross, Maurice was on common ground with Jowett and other exponents of the growing Abelardianism or exemplarism. But in his view of the divine wrath and his 'sense of the awfulness of God's nature and being' (p. 210) he stood apart from them. He was pointing the way beyond the false nineteenth-century dilemma, 'penal substitution or exemplarism', and anticipating the recovery of a more comprehensive doctrine. *The Doctrine of Sacrifice* brought back the unity of atonement and creation; it linked together the idea of sacrifice and the doctrine of the Trinity; it gave to many their first glimpse of the classic conception of the Cross as the divine victory. In our own day Aulen's exposition of the classic conception, Vincent Taylor's demonstration of the centrality of the idea of sacrifice in the

New Testament, Quick's synthesis of the classic conception and the idea of sacrifice, have done, by more
scientific theological methods, what Maurice did
intuitively and naïvely with a pre-critical technique of
Bible exposition.

III

The close connection between creation and redemption in Maurice's thought involved him in some
difficulty in his treatment of sin. He appeared to some
of his contemporaries to imply that the essence of
Atonement was that Christ revealed to men the truth
about themselves as created in the divine image: men
had been ignorant that sacrifice is the true meaning of
their lives, but now they know it and can act upon it.
It was a real difficulty. There are passages in *The Doctrine of Sacrifice* where atonement seems to be identified
with the giving to men of knowledge about God and
and their own nature which they did not possess
before; and there are passages in the *Life* where sin
seems to be identified with the refusal to believe that
we are not sinners but children of God. The biographer
was deeply distressed by a conversation between
McLeod Campbell and Shairp in which Campbell had
said, 'those who, like Maurice, regard Christ's work as
only taking away our alienation, by making us see the
Father's eternal good will towards us, as this only and
no more, they take no account of the sense of guilt in
man. According to their view there is nothing real in
the nature of things answering to this sense of guilt.
The sense of guilt becomes a mistake which further

knowledge removes. All sin is thus reduced to ignorance'.[1]

The biographer thought Campbell's remarks very unfair, and could hardly believe that they had been correctly reported. Yet there is a strain in Maurice's teaching which caused, and still causes, the reflection, 'Is sin then unreal?' Some of his statements are most perplexing when put side by side with the profound sense of sin and penitential self-abasement in his character. The problem is due, I think, to the tenacity with which he clings, here as in other parts of his teaching, to the principle of *Werde was du bist*, 'become what you are'. Men *are* in the divine image, men *are* members of a redeemed race, men *have* God as their Father. Sin is to act as if these things were not true, to slip into a false view of what things mean. To know how things really are—is to be delivered from sin. Yes: but the ignorance and the knowledge of which Maurice speaks in this connection are ignorance and knowledge not in the sense of the Board of Education or of the Utilitarians, but in the Biblical sense which gives the words a profound moral and spiritual content. We are *ignorant* of our relation to God because a deep self-centredness grips us with its idolatrous dominance: we *know* God only by a conversion of the whole man. And this conversion, while it involves a man owning himself a sinner, involves also his acknowledging that his status as God's son is the *real* thing about him. Maurice is certainly allowing his Platonism to affect his notion of things *real* and *unreal*. But his use of the

[1] *Life of F.D.M.*, II, p. 538.

word 'to know' is as certainly drawn from the Bible.

'No man', says Maurice, 'has a right to say "my race is a sinful fallen race", even when he confesses the greatness of his own sin and fall; because he is bound to contemplate his race in the Son of God.'[1] It is hard to hold some of Maurice's antinomies in a logical consistency; but in Maurice himself, at once a penitent and a Christian humanist, they formed one single whole. No one confessed more constantly 'the greatness of his own sin and fall', and no one more constantly strove 'to contemplate his race in the Son of God'.

[1] *Life of F.D.M.*, II, p. 408.

CHAPTER V

MAURICE AND MANSEL

I

On one of the Sundays early in 1858 Maurice was entertaining as preacher of Lincoln's Inn Dr Thomson, the future Archbishop of York, who had come up from Oxford for his sermon; and on the walk back to Russell Square he heard from his guest about the Bampton lectures which were being delivered during the term, and of the stir which they were causing to crowded audiences. Mr Mansel, afterwards Dean of St Paul's, was using a method of apologetic which many of the orthodox were hailing as a blow to the forces of infidelity. But Thomson described the lectures to Maurice as 'the most unalloyed Atheism that had been heard in England for generations'; and Maurice at once began and pursued to a point of exhaustion the fiercest of all his controversies.

No one nowadays reads Mansel's *The Limits of Religious Thought examined in eight lectures preached before the University of Oxford;* but the lectures are readable enough.[1] For crisp, clear, incisive English they leave Maurice's writings far behind; and there are

[1] A fresh estimate of them has been given by W. W. S. March in *Theology,* July 1942 ('Revised Reviews', xvii). An older treatment of the controversy is to be found in R. H. Hutton, *Essays, Theological and Literary,* I, ch. V.

few books which combine an argument about the limits of reason and moral judgment with so effective a religious appeal. The lectures are a defence of the Christian Revelation by the method of Christian Agnosticism. The limits of human thought about religion are akin to the limits of human thought in general. Since our minds are finite we can reach the conviction that an Infinite Being exists; but what the nature of that Infinite Being is we are powerless to know, and neither reason nor conscience can make any profitable speculations about it. The Christian Revelation does not give us the knowledge of God as He is in Himself, but such knowledge about Him as He has thought fit to disclose for the regulation of our lives and of our thoughts about Him. 'Speculative' knowledge of God cannot be: only 'regulative' knowledge about Him is possible. 'We must remain content with the belief that we have that knowledge of God which is best adapted to our wants and training. How far that knowledge represents God as He is, we know not, and we have no need to know.' The Revelation of God does not vindicate itself to us by considerations of moral or rational congruity: *our* ideas of what is moral or rational are too limited to be our guides in judging. No, the proper use for reason in connection with Revelation is simply the consideration of External Evidences. By Evidences of miracle and prophecy the Revelation is proved, and on the strength of the Evidences we accept it whole and entire. It matters not whether or no the dogma of the Trinity makes good sense philosophically, or whether the dogma of the Atonement fits or does not fit our own moral ideas. The dogmas are part of the Revelation which we accept, and we receive the Revelation and live by it with a response of the whole man.

Mansel does not part with the use of analogy, but he limits it severely. 'Reason does not deceive us, if we will only read her witness aright; and Reason herself gives us warning, when we are in danger of reading it wrong. The light that is within us is not darkness; only it cannot illuminate that which is beyond the sphere of its rays . . . The flaming sword turns every way against those who strive, in the strength of their own reason, to force their passage to the tree of life.' 'God did create the human manifestation of morality, when He created the moral constitution of man, and placed him in those circumstances by which the eternal principles of right and wrong are modified in relation to this present life.' But we have no right to assume 'that there is, if not a perfect identity, at least an exact resemblance between the moral nature of man and that of God; that nothing can be compatible with the boundless goodness of God, which is incompatible with the little goodness of which man may be conscious in himself'.

At a time when the *all*-sufficiency of human reason was being proclaimed by critics of the Christian faith and sometimes tacitly assumed by theologians there were many who welcomed the blow which Mansel seemed to be striking, and were unaware of how dangerous a boomerang it might prove to be. But the best judges were horrified at the lengths to which

Mansel had gone. Hort said 'He holds the doctrine of universal nescience more consciously and clearly than I suppose any other Englishman; a just nemesis on Butler's probabilities! So perish all half-way houses!'[1] John Stuart Mill's retort is famous, 'I will call no being good who is not what I mean when I apply that epithet to my fellow creatures, and if such being can sentence me to hell for not so calling him, to hell I will go'. Herbert Spencer, the prophet of the unknowable, claimed that his own Agnosticism was only carrying a step further the 'Christian Agnosticism' of Mansel: the adjective vanishing, the noun alone surviving!

II

Maurice was stung to a violence unparalleled in the whole of his life of conflict. Even his friends were perplexed by his violence and felt that it prevented him from letting his readers see calmly and clearly what the finer points of the discussion were. In a sense Maurice was throwing away an opportunity. He might have dealt with Mansel's errors with the technique of patience which he had used so successfully in the first portion of *The Kingdom of Christ*—exploring the half-truths behind the errors and showing that he understood them. But this was impossible. Mansel had touched, as with a sharp point, the nerve not only of Maurice's theology, but of Maurice's whole life. The life of a Christian is to *know* God, the Father, the Son and the Holy Ghost. If Mansel is right, then the life which Maurice lives is not life after all. It was not a

[1] *Life and letters of F. J. A. Hort*, I, p. 398.

discussion between the beliefs of Mansel and the beliefs of Maurice, so much as Maurice hurling his whole self in desperation against an argument of Mansel—and (so it seemed to him) a cold and rather cynical argument at that. Worse still, Mansel was winning the applause of those who shouted for orthodoxy and were ready to swallow uncritically *any* thesis which seemed to tell for orthodoxy at the moment. 'If the religious Press had not declared, almost *en masse*, in favour of Mansel, I would not have written against him.'

Maurice's chief writing in this controversy is *What is Revelation?* The first part of the book is a series of Sermons on the Epiphany. These, dealing with such subjects as the Coming of the Magi, St Paul at Athens, and the Signs in the Fourth Gospel, present, as effectively as sermons can, a single theme: that men can know God, and that they do so not by external evidences apart from a personal knowledge wrought in us by the Spirit. The Magi, in undertaking their journey, 'acted on the conviction that this was their duty. They opened their hearts to God's teaching, and He manifested His Son to them. He led them to the Child'. The signs recorded by St John 'are not arguments to convince the understanding that it ought to suspend its own proper exercises; they are unveilings or manifestations to the whole man, of the nature, character, mind of the Son of Man; and therefore, as He shows us in the passage of which my text forms a part, of the nature, character, mind of the Father who sent Him'. The sermons are among Maurice's best. But the larger part of the book consists of 'letters to a

Student of Theology on the Bampton Lectures of
Mr Mansel'. Maurice writes as to a pupil of Mansel's
sitting at his feet at Oxford; sarcasms abound, and the
'bedridden woman' argument is used once again. 'How
rude and poor my way of arriving at the force of a word
is, in comparison with Mr Mansel's . . . But you and I
are not Schoolmen; we are roughing it in the world.
We have to look upon all questions as they bear upon
the actual business of life.' 'I believe that among Mr
Mansel's auditors there will have been not a few on
whom his words will have acted as a most soothing
lullaby, who will have wrapped themselves in com-
fortable thankfulness that they were not Rationalists,
Spiritualists, or even as that German; who will have
rejoiced to think that they do not trouble themselves
about eternal things which are out of man's reach,
like Puritans and Methodists . . . such men, I believe,
do more to lower the moral tone and practice of
England than all sceptics and infidels altogether.'

Amid the violence of these letters Maurice's criticism of Mansel's doctrine unfolds itself. The Bible is
against Mansel, and must be rewritten if he is right. So
is a long line of saints, mystics and men of God, whose
characteristic language is blasphemy if Mansel is right.
Mansel substitutes a set of propositions, taught by the
Bible and the Church and accepted in bulk on the
strength of evidences, for that which underlies both the
Bible and the Church—namely the self-revelation to
our persons of a Person whom we come to know only
where external evidences are corroborated by an act
of divine grace within us. In short, Mansel is treating

the Christian Faith as 'a revealed religion'; whereas
Maurice believes not in 'natural religion' crowned by
'a revealed religion', but (without using these precise
terms) in the 'general revelation' and 'special revelation' of St Augustine. In combating the rationalism of
infidelity Mansel has succumbed to the rationalism of a
theology which, by identifying Reason and Understanding, does no justice to the possibilities of Reason
when it is informed by Faith. But the argument of
Maurice is broken again and again by impassioned
outbursts. 'I was beginning to comment on these
words. I was trying to tell you what impression they
left on me. I cannot. I can only say if they are true,
let us burn our Bibles, let us tell our countrymen that
the agony and bloody sweat of Christ, His cross and
passion, His death and burial, His resurrection and
ascension, mean nothing.'

III

This chapter is the shortest in this book because, of
all the episodes in Maurice's life, the Mansel controversy
is the one from which it is hardest to draw constructive theological material. A later work entitled *A
Sequel to What is Revelation* gave a quieter statement of
Maurice's case, but throughout the controversy
Maurice spoke and wrote in a way that recalls Julia
Wedgwood's description: 'His spirit felt the neigh-
bourhood of a great truth as a mighty magnet, and in
the rush with which he would turn towards it, the
sense of relevance would be submerged.'[1] Today a

[1] *Nineteenth Century Teachers*, p. 53.

student of the problems of Revelation and Reason
would read many volumes before he would be directed
to the Mansel controversy; and the episode is memorable chiefly as a mirror wherein are focused the character of Maurice as a Christian and the dominant
conviction of his whole life. The violence of his
reaction to Mansel, taking by surprise many even of
those who knew Maurice best, was the most signal
disclosure of how the conviction *quem nosse vivere* had
come to penetrate his whole being. R. H. Hutton
summed up the controversy thus: 'Dr Mansel conceived
that Christianity tells us just enough to keep us right
with a God whom we cannot really know; Mr Maurice
that the only way to be so kept right is by a direct and,
in its highest form, *conscious* participation in the very
life of God'.

A possible criticism of Maurice is that, on his own
principle of connecting theology with the personal
convictions of men, he was doing less than justice to
Mansel. Thinking Mansel's thesis to be a clever *tour-de-
force*, he did not pause to think that Mansel like himself
was speaking from a deep religious conviction concerning the nature of communion between God and
the human soul. There are some passages in the
Bamptons where Mansel's argument on the limitation
of human reason is mingled with an intuitive understanding of the meaning of the finite soul's adoration of
its creator. Mansel's work does here and there reproduce, amid an argument of much perversity, a factor
in man's relation to God which the Coleridgian theology did not always reproduce—the sense of adoring

dependence upon an inscrutable Wisdom, Majesty and Love. It is only applying the lesson of *The Kingdom of Christ* to say that Maurice's refutation of Mansel's thesis would have been the more effective if he had paused to recognize that religious perception which the Bamptons do disclose. There are passages[1] where, amid the description of the inability of the reason and the conscience to know God, Mansel is telling of how in fact the soul may be held fast in communion with God Himself. The same may be said—and not only by Barthians—of some passages in Karl Barth's exposition of the Epistle to the Romans.

It was a unique controversy. One aspect of it, however—the relation of events and propositions in the process of Revelation—remains as a live issue. While it requires for its solution the delicate instruments of the patient theologian, it frequently evokes the sledge-hammer of the prophet. When Christians become absorbed in a rationalism which turns the faith into a set of propositions there is need for the prophetic assertion that Christianity is a person in whom we believe. And when, conversely, Christians become absorbed self-consciously in the personal experience of a personal relation to God, there is need for an insistence (no less prophetic because it is intellectual) upon the objectivity of the pattern of the Faith. The Mansel controversy saw Maurice as the prophet in the first of these causes: but there were times in his life when he had to espouse the latter cause against evangelical pietism. He knew Him whom he believed, for

[1] Cf. for example pp. 264-9.

he knew also the importance both of the events wherein He was revealed and of the propositions in which the meaning of the events are set forth. Nor was he unmindful of the Biblical *images*, whose place in the process of revelation has been the theme of some very recent Bampton lectures. Though he nowhere discussed the significance of images, his own teaching constantly shews their importance.

CHAPTER VI

THE HOLY SCRIPTURES

I

THE conflict within the Church of England concerning the truth and authority of the Bible came to a head in the decade which followed the expulsion of Maurice from King's College. In 1859 Darwin's *Origin of Species* was published; in 1860 *Essays and Reviews* and in 1862 the first portion of the *Commentary upon the Pentateuch* by Bishop Colenso of Natal. Faith seemed to be in the melting-pot. Darwin had shaken the credibility of the special creation of Man, Colenso was challenging the historical character of the stories of the patriarchs, Moses and the Exodus. Was the Bible true? We can realize that the issue was commonly presented with much crudity when we learn that a clergyman destined for the Episcopal bench wrote a preface to a work entitled *Moses or the Zulu*.[1]

Maurice was handicapped in the giving of guidance to his fellow churchmen in their distress. He was frankly not interested in science: 'he ignored it', says Julia Wedgwood, 'almost completely; and he was saved from any real antagonism to that movement of thought which is vaguely called Darwinism by understanding it as little as a traveller newly arrived in some

[1] I owe this reference to C. H. Smyth in *The Genius of the Church of England* (S.P.C.K. 1947), p. 58.

distant land understands the purport of its most idiomatic and hurried conversation'. Similarly he had only a perfunctory interest in questions of historical criticism. To the liberals therefore he could be of little use as guide, philosopher and friend, and they offended him by seeming to offer a set of religious ideas in place of the living God of the Biblical revelation. To the orthodox he had long been a dangerous heretic, and now their policy of fear and suppression outraged him. So he writes, 'I feel how hopeless it is to extract any theology or humanity from the *Essays and Reviews*. But I cannot think that the fears which are expressed of them betoken much confidence in the Bible or in God. One can only hope that the discussion may lead us to seek a deeper foundation than the essayists or their opponents appear to deem necessary'.[1]

Today if we are in sight of the 'deeper foundation' we may learn something of it from Maurice's own approach to the use and the authority of the Bible. Despite the handicaps in his equipment he was discovering that foundation himself. And he kept his head: 'we will allow God', he says, 'to take care of His own ark the Church and that which it contains, without supposing that we can make it safer or steadier by stretching our own clumsy hands to keep it from falling'.

II

Maurice's teaching upon the authority of the Bible, in so far as he ever puts it into anything like a systematic shape, is to be found in his earliest and in one of his

[1] *Life of F.D.M.*, II, p. 384.

latest works: first, in *The Kingdom of Christ*; and second, in *Claims of the Bible and of Science*, published in 1863 with Colenso specially in view. Both books give a consistent view of some principles to which Maurice adhered throughout.

As regards *the meaning of Inspiration*, Maurice insisted that divine inspiration is as wide in its operations as the created world. Everything that is well done betokens inspiration. 'Every man who is doing the work that he is set to do may believe that he is inspired with a power to do that work.' Nowhere does Maurice make this point more triumphantly than in a Sermon on Balaam. Here, he says, is a heathen seer, outside the covenant and corrupt in his motives—yet under inspiration from God he prophesied the truth. And Maurice, noting that it is the year of the Great Exhibition (the sermon was in 1851) quotes with satisfaction a statement by the Archbishop of Canterbury: 'Knowledge of every kind which leads to the creation of railways and steam-carriages, as well as the most spiritual, is of God, from the inspiration of the Most High'. 'We need', says Maurice, 'to proclaim this truth which was never more needed to preserve nations from sinking into atheism, in proportion as they become stewards of ampler treasures and mightier powers.'

Yet a diffused inspiration is not the whole story. The Bible is *not as other Books*. And the distinction lies not in the fact of the Biblical writers being inspired, but in what they were doing. 'The question is not, were these men who wrote the Scriptures inspired by God? but, were they in a certain position and appointed to a certain work?' They were. They lived within a divine kingdom in history made by God, and they had the unique office of being set by God to proclaim that kingdom. The uniqueness of the Bible as inspired lies in the uniqueness of the Biblical history as the history of a Kingdom of God in the midst of the world. And as Israel was what no other people was, and as Israel's history is as no other history, so the books which God bade men in Israel write for a testimony to His Kingdom are what no other books are. Such is the special character of the Bible. Maurice is prepared to accept the phrase 'verbal inspiration', for thought and language are so interwoven that to inspire the thought is to inspire the words: they cannot be sharply distinguished. But Maurice is unable to accept the definition of the Bible as the 'Word of God'. The identification is unscriptural; nowhere does the Bible tell us that it is the 'Word of God'—it is a slogan of orthodoxy not sanctioned by the Scriptures themselves.

The *Biblical history* is therefore the crux of Maurice's theory. Upon the uniqueness of the history the special character of Scripture rests. But is the history true? Prove it to be false, and the theory will collapse; for all depends not upon the Bible as a special sort of book or upon the writers as possessors of a special sort of inspiration, but upon the history as a special sort of history. So we can see how unfortunate was Maurice's lack of training in historical criticism. Not that he neglected it altogether. In *The Kingdom of Christ* he had dealt with such questions as the discrepancies between the four gospels, and in face of these questions he had considered the difference between the writing of history and the chronicling of events, and he had argued that the investigation of events cannot properly be separated from the interpretation of them. Similarly in *The Unity of the New Testament* he had tried to deal with the thesis of the Tübingen school of criticism by demonstrating the unity of theological and religious outlook to be found in the books of the New Testament despite their differences. But neither of these discussions did he carry very far or treat at all thoroughly.

It was in the Colenso crisis that Maurice's conception of the Biblical history was severely tested. Colenso and Maurice had been kindred spirits, and at the time of the troubles leading to Maurice's expulsion from King's College, Colenso had dedicated a volume to him. Now Maurice felt the legal proceedings against Colenso to be intolerable, but he broke with him decisively on the theological issue. We find him writing to Sir Edward Strachey: 'There has been an estrangement between Colenso and me since he came to England. I think the Bible is the great deliverer from ecclesiastical bondage . . . But when he took up the exactly opposite maxim, when he treated the Bible as itself the instrument of our slavery, and seemed to think that to throw it off would be a great step to emancipation, I felt that he was giving up the ground to Dr Pusey and the Bishop of Oxford . . . I saw nothing before us but that fanaticism against criticism . . . which those last few years had developed . . . But if I identified myself with those liberal thinkers, I must have

abandoned my own position. To make Colenso understand this is impossible at present: and if I met him at
your house, I suspect we should only embarrass each
other and embarrass you.'[1]

Claims of the Bible and of Science is a series of letters on
the Colenso controversy. Maurice speaks strongly of
the rights of critical study and of the mistake involved
in fearing Darwinism: but, having done that, he hits
Colenso hard. Colenso says that the Pentateuch is not
history; and that because Moses is not the author and
the books contain inconsistencies in the arithmetic of
populations and in dates and geography, therefore we
ought to look to the Pentateuch not for history but for
'religious ideas'. But what is history? Colenso is con-
fusing history and arithmetic: 'Numerical facts are
admittedly important, but they do not constitute
history; they do not even constitute the evidence of
history. A very great exaggeration in numbers in the
account of the expedition of Xerxes may make me
doubt the information or even the veracity of Hero-
dotus; it will not make me doubt the battle of Salamis'.
So, for all that Colenso can prove, what lies behind the
Pentateuch may still not be religious ideas, but events
—and in particular the event of God's deliverance of
Israel from slavery in Egypt, an event which gave her
her sense of election and the conviction that God had
mightily directed her course. Some such event
accounts for there being a Pentateuch at all, and
Colenso has not demolished the core of history.

Maurice now turns about. On the other side are

[1] *Life of F D.M.* II p. 486.

those who suppose that if the chronicling of detailed events in the Pentateuch is in any way imperfect or if the writer is proved to be in any way fallible, then the historical basis of Israel's story and the inspired char- inspired character of the books disappears. He is scath- ing at the expense of those who consider the Mosaic authorship to be vital, using the very Maurician argument that to stake so much upon a fallible, human figure in the narratives is to ascribe to fallible agents an impor- tance which the Bible itself never ascribes to them. Here as elsewhere Maurice was being too facile, and indeed he was more than facile in his treatment of particular historical problems. He thinks it probable that there was a limited Deluge over a portion of the earth. He thinks it probable that a historical Eden existed, and might before long be vindicated by archaeology: if not, he can accept the loss without dismay. All this is clumsy. He remains an amateur in historical science. But he will not budge from his contention that history is what matters in the Bible; and that, with a right view of the nature of historical evidence, we can find in the Bible a core of history which Colenso has not demolished. Finally he ends the series of letters by putting two men side by side: Colenso, Bishop of Natal, and Lee, Bishop of Manchester, who had defended the wrong view of Bible history with the wrong arguments. 'Here', says Maurice, 'we have a remarkable illustration of the danger to which we are exposed on both sides . . . unbelief in the divine word is as much the disease of the Bishop of Manchester as it is of the Bishop of Natal. In both there is the denial of

Him who is and was and is to come, of His government over the ages that are gone, and over the ages now . . . their opinions both scandalize me: I could not hold either and be a minister of the English Church. But, thank God, I am not a standard for either of them: I am not called to be a judge.'

The naïveté of Maurice's handling of the controversy is obvious. But he was being prophetic: Biblical study has come to affirm that, though criticism has destroyed the reliability of the Bible as a chronicle, it is none the less divine acts in history—and not ideas—which made the Bible to be what it is. And he was, for all the clumsiness of his handling of the problem of history, putting his finger upon an important point concerning the nature of history and historical evidence. It *is* valid evidence for a great event, that a nation's litera-ture and religious experience took a certain shape, and that an event must be postulated such as created this shape.[1] R. H. Hutton put the point at issue thus: 'Colenso thought he could distinguish the untrust-worthiness of a history sufficiently by bringing to light a great number of minor discrepancies in it. Maurice thought he could distinguish its trustworthiness as regards its main features by comparing the moral and spiritual antecedents in one page of the history with the moral and spiritual consequents in another, and show-ing how truly they correspond to each other, and how full of human nature, and how fully verified by our own experience, was the connection between the different

---

[1] Cf. the recent treatment of the problem of the Exodus on these lines by Dr Wheeler-Robinson, *The History of Israel*, pp. 224-8.

stages. For my part I believe that both are right up to a certain point, but that Maurice has got hold of immeasurably the more important criterion of the two.'[1]

The points which Maurice was making were lost in the fog of battle. The orthodox thought that they saw things crystal clear: either the Bible was true or it was not; and those questions of Maurice, 'what do you mean by true?', 'what do you mean by history?', were not being faced. And, while Maurice abhorred the theological outlook of Colenso, his abhorrence of the proceedings against him, his belief that critical studies ought to be pursued and his inability to call the Bible the 'Word of God' put him alongside the Radicals in current estimation. Pusey and Shaftesbury joined hands against heresy: the hunt was up; and the fatal manifesto of 1871 (known commonly as the Oxford Declaration), signed by thousands of the clergy and the laity, denounced together those who deny the Bible to be the Word of God and those who deny the everlasting punishment of the wicked. The problem remained.

III

Did Maurice himself indicate that 'deeper foundation' whose need he saw so clearly? I believe that his own use of the Bible as an expositor, throughout his whole ministry, was laying bare that foundation in a remarkable way. 'I do not think', he said, 'that we have had the courage to bring out the Scriptures of the Old and New Testament in their simple, clear sense as a

[1] *Modern Guides of English Thought in Matters of Faith*, p. 337.

revelation of God to men or as a lamp to the feet of us Englishmen in the nineteenth century'.[1] But he *had* the courage himself; and, if the nineteenth century was slow to understand him, the mid-twentieth century may be more ready to sit at his feet.

The study of Maurice's exposition of Scripture is a huge task. My own investigations allow me to give only a kind of interim report, drawn chiefly from *Patriarchs and Lawgivers of the Old Testament*, *Prophets and Kings of the Old Testament*, *The Unity of the New Testament*, *The Gospel of St John*, and the very Biblical *Sermons on the Prayer Book*. What are the prominent themes of Maurice's Biblical teaching?

Patriarchs and Lawgivers shows Maurice at the height of his power in expounding some very characteristic ideas. The Fall of Man was a real event, but it is not the centre of theology: for, despite the Fall, the divine image in Man persists and in the stories of the patriarchs its persistence is discernible. The divine order of creation 'has not been interrupted because a man has refused obedience to it;—it is only made more evident by that violation . . . Man has set up a self-will, has fallen under the dominion of the nature which God had given him. This very act is a step in his education—a means by which God will teach him more fully what he is, what he is not, what he was meant to be, and what he was not meant to be; how he may thwart the purposes of his Creator, and how he may conspire with them' (p. 61). Hence the Deluge: 'He uses the powers of Nature to destroy those who had made

[1] From the Preface to *Patriarchs and Lawgivers of the Old Testament*.

themselves the slaves of Nature. The laws under which
He has established the earth become the means of its
purification, and of the punishment of those who have
misused it' (p. 65). So too the floods, famines,
pestilences of which we read are not unrelated to the
Divine Government of the world: they belong to 'the
history of an actual education; a government of voluntary creatures to teach them subjection;—an education
of voluntary creatures to make them free' (p. 63).

The mighty acts of deliverance and judgment in
Israel are therefore not isolated wonders or favours:
they are the assertions of the divine kingdom against
human rebellions, and of the divine law of liberty
against human tyrants. The story of the Kingdom of
God in Israel, with its incidents concerning good and
bad kingship and human justice, is related to the conception of the kingdom over the created world and
finally to the kingdom proclaimed by Christ in the
Gospels. Here the miracles of Christ are in line with
the same divine method. They were wrought not to
prove His divinity by their abnormality, but to assert
the claim and the character of the Kingdom of God
against the abnormalities of human sin and of diabolical
interference with the created world.

This conception of the Kingdom of a God who is
always and at once Creator, Redeemer and Judge
explains the unity of the two Testaments. Seldom has
the unity of Law and Gospel been shown so clearly.
The Gospel, in overthrowing the Law as a means of
salvation, reaffirms the validity of the law as a revelation of the moral structure of the world. By bringing

us within the redeemed life of the new creation the Gospel opens our eyes to perceive the foundation of law upon which the world rests, and to be more than ever aware of its imperative character. Prayer-Book revisers who are anxious to exclude the closing verses of the *Venite*, the Ten Commandments and the Commination service might study what Maurice has to say on each of these in his *Sermons on the Prayer Book*.

Believing in the unity of the two Testaments, Maurice employed the principle of Scripture interpreting Scripture. As early as 1830 he mentioned a sermon by Mr Irving which 'expounded one part of Scripture by another in a way that I never remember to have heard before. An assertion of his, that the Old Testament is the dictionary of the New, threw a light upon some things which had been puzzling me very much, and I think is quite a guiding light in all Biblical studies'.[1] Though Maurice used this principle extensively, he used it with caution. Discussing the question of Old Testament typology he deprecates certain ways of employing it, 'because I am afraid it is apt to beget a feeling that the Bible is not so much a real book containing a history of actual men, as a repository of ingenious analogies . . . But the great truth which is implied in this typical view of Scripture, I have endeavoured to illustrate in each discourse. Because I regard Abraham, Joseph and Jacob as actual men, men made in the image of God, I must regard them as showing forth some aspect of His character and life whom I recognize as the express image of God's

[1] *Life of F.D.M.*, I, p. 107.

person'.[1] Hence, without any of the extravagances which sometimes appear in typological exegesis, Maurice's exposition of some of the Old Testament characters is full of Christ: not through subtle correspondences of phrase and detail, but through the likeness of Christ's image in those who were His prototypes. Maurice believed that Christ was at work in the history of Israel; the Word was with the chosen people for centuries before He became Incarnate in their midst.

And when, lastly, He became Incarnate, He came not as a stranger into a foreign country but as the Creator into His own. This point is drawn out again and again in the Commentary upon the Gospel of St John. 'John's is emphatically the Christian Gospel, exhibiting the relation of Christ as the Head of humanity to Christ as the Son of God.' 'They were looking for a king who should reign over men; they did not think that this king must be One who had from the beginning been the light of men.' 'Christ was not a King whom a faction was to set up. He was the original Lord of men, ruling not as a stranger, but as One possessing the most intimate knowledge of that which is distinct and peculiar in each man, and of the man that is in each.'

To this principle of *Christus Consummator* Maurice always returns as one drawn by a magnet. And as a result he was accused of finding his favourite ideas in Scripture, of being one-sidedly Johannine, and of pressing the exegesis of books and passages into a sort of Maurician scheme. There is some justice in the complaint, for the thought of Maurice seldom wandered

[1] *Patriarchs and Lawgivers*, p. 152.

for long from the doctrines of the Johannine prologue.
Yet he was a man of the whole Bible, for his world was
always the Bible world. It was not the illusory world
of some of his Victorian contemporaries, but the
world of the deluge and the plagues, of ruined cities
and exiled nations. If we have come to see that the
world is like this, then Maurice's use of the Bible
speaks to us in a fresh way.

The expositor of Scripture is faced with the problem
of how to show the contemporary significance of the
books which he is expounding. Maurice felt that the
usual methods of doing this were unsatisfactory, since
they involved partly the dismissing of the Bible as
irrelevant to our own very different times and partly
the 'picking' from it of moral maxims and exhorta-
tions.[1] It cannot be said that he worked out an
alternative conception at all fully, but the ideal he held
in view might be described in the words of Professor
Dodd in his Inaugural Lecture at Cambridge: 'Our
task is not thus to pick and choose, but to grasp the
whole first-century Gospel in its temporary, historical
and therefore actual reality, and then to make the
bold and even perilous attempt to translate the whole
into contemporary terms.'[1] Perhaps Maurice's most
notable attempt to do this was in his *Lectures on the
Apocalypse* (1861). Babylon, the harlot city, is—
London. 'If, again, in this city there is, in clergy and
laity, in the idle and the busy, the noble, the trades-
man, the artisan, on one plea or another, upon religious

---

[1] *Patriarchs and Lawgivers*, pp. xvii–xviii.
[1] C. H. Dodd, *The Present Task in New Testament Studies*, 1936.

or irreligious pretexts, a disposition to reverence the visible more than the invisible, the traditions of society more than moral and eternal laws—if this disposition has gained great power, and threatens to become supreme, then it is also a true instinct which recalls the greatness of Babylon, when we are tempted to exult in the greatness of London, and foretells that the one may not be stabler than the other.' 'We have found Babylon in the Papacy; we have forgotten to look for it in ourselves. We have not seen that the harlotry of sense is at work everywhere.' But what is apostasy? 'We forget that we *stand off from* that which is our proper standing-ground; that if we revolt it is from a government which is actually established over us . . . There could not have been an apostasy if there had not been a Kingdom of God set up in the world . . . For this, I believe, lies at the root of all our moral evils, that we do not confess humanity to be married to Christ; all men to have been claimed as citizens of His kingdom, and not of the Babel kingdom. We do not really confess that God has reconciled the world to Himself; therefore we do not really repudiate the world's assertion that it is separate from God, and that it can live without Him.'

IV

The history of Biblical theology since Maurice's day has indicated the prophetic character of his work. His limitations in criticism and science prevented him from contributing as he might to the needs of his own day and to the needs of the succeeding decades; but his

Biblical teaching points beyond those decades to the recovery of the Bible which is happening today.

It has been a confused story. There was first the need to assert the rights of critical study, and here Maurice did much to kindle the temper in which Hort and his Cambridge colleagues did their work. Then there came the gradual awareness that criticism could have its own wrong presuppositions and could lose the key to the Bible. And more recently there came the violent reactions in which a theological approach to the Bible has been recovered, and the labours of historical criticism have sometimes been disparaged in the supposed interests of the transcendental Word of God. Today Maurice may help us, for he foreshadows the synthesis which we are seeking. The Bible is the Book of the Divine Kingdom: it yields its secrets only to those who share its faith, and yet by the reality of its own human element it vindicates the role of the historical critic. Its climax is the Gospel, but the Gospel stands upon the ground-base of the creation, the covenant with Noah, and the giving of the Law to Moses; and as we are redeemed into the family of the Son of God we are enabled to perceive beneath our catastrophic world a foundation of which the same Son of God is the maker and builder.

CHAPTER VII

MAURICE THEN AND NOW

I

THE intervention of Maurice in the Colenso controversy had been prompted by an appeal from Sir Thomas
Acland, who wrote to him: 'For more than a quarter
of a century you have been helping Englishmen to see
through the theories and systems which have been
invented to prop up, restore, develop or narrow the
ancient edifice of their national Church; and, amidst
ceaseless contumely and misrepresentation levelled
against yourself, you have striven to teach, as Alexander Knox and S. T. Coleridge taught before you,
that the Bible and the Church of England can best bear
witness for their own truth, and for God's providence,
against infidelity and Pantheism.'[1] It had been a life of
conflict; but it was beginning to reap the gratitude of
those whom it had helped to a firmer faith, and its
closing years began to know a measure of peace.

In 1860 Palmerston had appointed Maurice to the
cure of St Peter's, Vere Street. There, as at Lincoln's
Inn, his ministry drew a congregation of both eminent
and humble folk; and they were utterly bewildered
by his attempt to resign on an unintelligibly scrupulous
point of conscience in 1862. In 1866 he was given the

[1] *Life of F.D.M.*, vol. II, p. 451.

Professorship of Moral Philosophy at Cambridge. Here he found a rest which he had never known before, away from the scenes of conflict in London. For a time he kept on his charge at Vere Street as well, travelling up from Cambridge to preach: but after a few years the double task proved too great for him, and he resigned the London church. In his farewell sermon to a crowded congregation the text was 'Plead thou my cause, O Lord, with them that strive with me, and fight thou against them that fight against me'; but the enemies he spoke of were not his theological foes, but his own sins. 'These are my foes, if I have courage to pray that God would fight against them in me, I must believe that He will fight against them in you.' In Cambridge we are told of the peace which he was finding. 'The rush of his start for a walk was now gone. His movements had, like his life, become quiet and measured . . . There was a beauty which seemed to shine round him, and was commonly observed by those among whom he was. It made undergraduates, not specially impressionable, stop and watch him.' His pastoral spirit led him to add to his Professorship the unpaid post of Chaplain of St Edward's Church, and there he preached, and catechized the children on Sunday afternoons. He looks back on the conflict he has been through; and he sums it up: 'I have laid a great many addled eggs in my time, but I think I see a connection through it all which I have only lately begun to realize. The desire for unity and the search for unity, both in the nation and in the Church, has haunted me all my days.'

The life in Cambridge was only for six years. Maurice died on Easter Monday 1872, while he was waiting for his friend and disciple Llewellyn Davies to celebrate Holy Communion by his sick-bed. His last conversation was 'about the Communion being for all peoples and nations . . . and about it being the work of women to teach men its meaning'. His last words were those of the Trinitarian blessing.

In looking for the fruit of Maurice's teaching it is natural to turn first to those who had shared with him the obloquy of Christian socialism. This subject has not been neglected by historians. Suffice it to say here that by the close of the century the typical Anglican view of the relation between religion and questions of the social order had undergone a very big change. And among the causes a special place belongs not to a direct influence of Maurice so much as to a diffused influence which passed from him through the more popular and intelligible energies of Charles Kingsley.

'To your works', wrote Kingsley to Maurice, 'I am indebted for the foundation of any coherent view of the word of God, of the Church of England, and the spiritual phenomena of the present and past ages.' With no more than a fraction of Maurice's intellectual powers, but with something of genius as pastor, preacher and humanist and with an interest in natural science almost unique among the clergy of the day, Kingsley strove to break some of the barriers between the sacred and the secular. He could be guilty of the greatest crudities in theology and of the *naïvetés* about democracy and progress which Maurice vehemently rejected. But he was vigorous, and he was intelligible. And to him, perhaps, more than to any single person it is due that many churchmen came both to shed their fear of Darwinism and to regard the movement of social emancipation as not unconnected with the Christian faith.

The different attitudes of Maurice and Kingsley towards democracy arose from their theology. Kingsley, for all his other-worldliness, could fall headlong into the crudest blurring of the line which divides the Divine Kingdom and a social utopianism. When Eleanor, Lady Ellerton, the heroine of *Alton Locke*, converts the Chartist tailor-poet from infidelity to Christianity, she says to him: 'That state, that city, Jesus said, was come, was now within us, had we eyes to see. And it is come. Call it the Church, the Gospel, civilization, freedom, democracy, association, what you will—I shall call it by the name which my Master spoke it—the name which includes all these and more than these—the Kingdom of God . . . In every age it has, sooner or later, claimed the steps of civilization, the discoveries of science, as God's inspiration, not men's inventions. It is now ready, if we may judge by the signs of the times, once again to penetrate, to convert, to recognize the political and social life of England, perhaps of the world; to vindicate democracy as the will and gift of God.' In this harangue we see Kingsley's enthusiasm, and mental confusion. Maurice would not have written this. His Christian socialism involved no blindness to the more stern and catastrophic aspects of the Kingdom in the Bible. If he

knew that God inspires, he knew also that Satan cor-
rupts and that judgment falls.

II

Maurice died a Cambridge Professor, and it was at
Cambridge that his theology bore the most direct fruit.
Hort had long been his disciple. As a nineteen-year-old
undergraduate he read *The Kingdom of Christ*. 'Though I
proceed very slowly indeed with it, every day seems to
bring out more clearly in my mind the truth, wisdom,
scripturality, and above all unity of Maurice's baptismal
scheme . . . I love him more and more every day.'[1]
And shortly before Hort returned from parish work to
Cambridge he said, 'Mr Maurice has been a dear friend
to me for twenty-three years, and I have been deeply
influenced by his books. To myself it seems that I owe
to them chiefly a firm and full hold of the Christian
faith'.[2] Hort came to make his home in St Peter's
Terrace in Cambridge in March 1872, eagerly looking
forward to having Maurice as a near neighbour; but
Maurice left Cambridge for the last time on the day of
Hort's arrival and died a few days later.

The debt of Hort to Maurice is indicated by some
seventy passages in Hort's *Life and Letters*, with many
comments on Maurice's expositions of Scripture. The
disciple was aware of some of the foibles of the master;
he once uses a coined verb *maurikizein*, and the context shows that it means to make 'a general attack on
the whole religious world of all parties'. But the point

[1] *Life and Letters of F. J. A. Hort*, I, p. 67.
[2] Ibid. II, p. 155.

where Hort's own work best shows the spirit and temper of Maurice is his Hulsean lectures for 1871, *The Way, the Truth, the Life*. Coleridge and Maurice alike are echoed when Hort says, 'The truth of God revealed in Christ calls not for the separate exercise of a unique faculty, but for the co-operation of every power by which we can read ourselves, and hold converse with whatever is not ourselves. Christian theology has in it indeed an element which other knowledge has not; but it embraces all elements that are scattered elsewhere.'[1] Maurice's mind is similarly apparent in sentences like these: 'It is not too much to say that the Gospel itself can never be fully known till nature as well as man is fully known; and that the manifestation of nature as well as man in Christ is part of His manifestation of God. As the Gospel is the perfect introduction to all truth, so on the other hand it is itself known only in proportion as it is used for the enlightenment of departments of truth which seem at first sight to lie beyond its boundaries.'[2] Hort's lectures are perhaps the most complete expression of the doctrine of *Christus Consummator*: they have a clarity and a precision of Biblical exegesis which Maurice's work never attained, but they are Maurician in their power to embrace the widest field of doctrine within the exposition of a single passage of St John. 'A life devoted to truth is a life of vanities abased and ambitions foresworn': Maurice and Hort were not the only scholars of the time to exemplify these words, but each

[1] *The Way, the Truth, the Life*, p. 76.
[2] Ibid. p. 83.

of them did exemplify them in a way peculiarly his own.

Of Westcott's relation to Maurice it is difficult to speak quite so definitely. It was as late as 1852 that Hort wrote to Westcott: 'Certainly I cannot but be pleased at your having bought (and, may it be hoped? read) Maurice's *Kingdom of Christ*, for you seem to me to have misunderstood his position and objects.'[1] We do not know what this reproach refers to, and a little later in the correspondence we read that the book was still unread. Though Westcott paid a tribute to Maurice's *Social Morality* in the preface to his own *Social Aspects of Christianity* and on another occasion referred to that work of Maurice as one of his 'very few favourite books',[2] Dr Moore Ede tells of a conversation in which Westcott said that apart from 'one book' he avoided reading Maurice, for 'I felt his way of thinking was so like my own, that if I read Maurice I should endanger my originality'.[3] The kinship of ideas was apparent to Westcott when in 1884 he says of Maurice's biography, 'I never knew before how deep my sympathy is with most of his characteristic thoughts. It is most refreshing to read such a book, such a life'.[4]

It may seem surprising that the Cambridge School of Theology in the seven and more decades since Maurice's death has not been more conscious of him as a creative force behind its work. The fact is explainable. Partly, the pre-critical point of view of Maurice's Biblical work made it seem obsolete during the years

[1] *Life and Letters of F. J. A. Hort*, I, p. 222.
[2] *Life and Letters of B. F. Westcott*, II, p. 160.
[3] *The Modern Churchman*, xxiii, p. 527.
[4] *Life and Letters of B. F. Westcott*, II, p. 37.

in which the critical study of the New Testament documents was the prevailing interest. Partly, the work of the Cambridge School became absorbed in the problems of criticism and exegesis with a tendency to disregard those wider questions concerning the interpretation of the Christian faith to which Maurice devoted himself. But if these wider questions are disregarded the understanding of the Bible itself suffers. Hort was aware of this, as his Hulsean lectures show; and if a new awareness of this is apparent in Cambridge studies today,[1] the significance of Maurice will become recognized once more. It is hard to doubt that, while he would never have been ready to abandon the primacy of Biblical studies and of the disciplines which they require, he would have welcomed the recent revision of the Theological Tripos whereby both philosophy and the later phases of Christian thought are given a larger scope. The 'Cambridge School' has come to mean Lightfoot, Hort, Westcott and those who succeeded them in their own tasks; but perhaps the final verdict of history will recognize a 'Cambridge School' which begins with Hare and Maurice and reaches beyond the specific labours of the great Trio into an era when theology will recover the wider range which Maurice believed it to possess.

III

It was less easy for the influence of Maurice to penetrate the successors of the Tractarians. Liddon followed

[1] Cf. the reference to the importance of Maurice made by Professor J. M. Creed in his Inaugural Lecture, 'The Study of the New Testament' *Journal of Theological Studies*, Jan.-April, 1941.

Pusey's attitude and could only say of Maurice, 'That so good a man should be mistaken is a very perplexing mystery of the moral world . . . No doubt he is a rebuke to most of us who hold truths which he denies. Tyre and Sidon have always a lesson for Chorazin and Bethsaida'.[1] Dean Church took a different view. As a very young graduate he had come to respect Maurice's mind, and his tribute to Maurice after his death[2] was a kind of prophecy of the final flowing together of Maurice's theology and the churchmanship of the successors of the Tractarians.

This flowing together of two streams which at first seemed divergent is to be seen in the remarkable story of Stewart Headlam, the first to combine the roles of Christian socialist and ritualistic priest. Headlam was an undergraduate at Cambridge during Maurice's professorship. 'It was his theology which drew me to Maurice at first. He believed in the old term of theology, and disliked any substitution for it of the word religion. It is easy to imagine what good news his teaching as to eternal life and eternal punishment was to such of us as had been terrified by the reiteration of the doctrine that half the world or more was condemned to future torment . . . Not that his teaching as to eternal life was the most important part of his teaching. That was the Fatherhood of God, with, as its corollary, the eternal Sonship of Christ and consequently the brotherhood of Man. It was from the doctrines of the Incarnation and the Atonement that he

---

[1] *Life of Henry Parry Liddon*, p. 74.
[2] R. W. Church, *Occasional Papers*, II, pp. 320–6.

derived what unifies his social teaching . . . In certain directions I may have gone further than Maurice went in his day—thus in my devotion to the Sacrament of the Altar—though not further, perhaps, than he would have gone had he been alive today.'[1] Headlam was devoted to Maurice. He tells of the crowds of 'horsey men' who flocked to Kingsley's lectures on history, while only a handful went to Maurice on moral philosophy: and Maurice's shyness impeded the sort of relationship which Headlam would have liked.

But Headlam's devotion remained, surviving the disapproval of Dean Vaughan, who disliked his 'doves' repeating Maurice's jargon, and of Bishop Jackson of London, who delayed Headlam's ordination to the priesthood on account of his aggressive Mauricisms. The upshot was that Headlam carried into his parish work, his labours with the Church-and-Stage Guild and his foundation of the Guild of St Matthew the principles of Maurice's teaching. The Guild's objects tell a tale of theological synthesis: they were, (1) to get rid by every possible means of the existing prejudices, especially on the part of Secularists, against the Church, her sacraments and doctrines, and to endeavour 'to justify God to the people'. (2) To promote frequent and reverent worship in the Holy Communion and a better observance of the teaching of the Church of England, as set forth in the Book of Common Prayer. (3) To promote the study of social and political questions in the light of the Incarnation. Headlam invented on the one hand the slogan 'It is the

[1] Quoted in F. G. Bettany, *Stewart Headlam: a Biography*, p. 20.

Mass that matters', and propagated on the other hand not only Maurice's 'Socialism' but also his belief that Biblical criticism need not be feared.[1]

Headlam is important as a sympton of something which was happening in more ways than can be traced in exact sequence. It is hard to distinguish precisely the cross-currents which led to the *Lux Mundi* school of the eighties and nineties. The biographies of the *Lux Mundi* men seldom refer to Maurice, and their conscious indebtedness was chiefly to T. H. Green. But Holland had been influenced by Stewart Headlam, and Gore by Westcott; and it is interesting to learn that Illingworth advised a student of philosophy (as lately as 1905) to begin with Maurice's *Moral and Metaphysical Philosophy*.[2] *Lux Mundi* sees Catholic theology no longer standing on the defensive against the spirit of the age, but incorporating it by the principle of the Incarnate Logos. Whereas the Tractarians resisted contemporary criticism and philosophy as incompatible with an authoritative divine revelation, the writers of *Lux Mundi* regarded their compatibility as a main assumption. 'Evolution was accepted as the work of the Logos through whom all things were made. It followed, among other things, that man's historical development, including that of the present age, is part of the creative movement of the Word, and therefore manifests His

---

[1] 'You may really hold what opinion you like about the Flood, or Balaam's ass, or Jonah and the whale, or the advisability of women coming to Church without their bonnets. The Church's belief that Moses, Isaiah or St Paul were inspired must be associated with her clear assertion that all good men are inspired.' S. D. Headlam, *The Service of Humanity*, p. 129.

[2] Cf. *Life of J. R. Illingworth*, p. 244.

light. Democracy, which characterizes the present era, can thus be seen as interpreting the worth of personality and the brotherhood of man. Socialism, again viewed as an existing tendency, illuminates the idea of authority in so far as this involves a rightful claim of the whole upon the part. But only the Incarnation, . . . together with its extension in the Church and the Sacraments, is adequate to interpret and validate the life of the individual and of society. The *Lux Mundi* theology is thus of one piece with the *Lux Mundi* sociology; and in both aspects it completes the Tractarian beginnings.'[1] It completed the mission of Tractarianism, however, only by introducing modifications which were deeply shocking to survivors of the older school such as Liddon. But if the modifications were in part the result of Hegelian influence, they were in part the outcome of a Johannine teaching on lines akin to those of Maurice.

It would be a mistake to think that all the theologians of this school were concerned with the social corollaries of their teaching. But both the theology and the sociology set us asking whether Maurice, if he could have had a glimpse of the closing years of the century, would not have seen at least a part of the fruit of his conflicts. The theology of *Lux Mundi* saw the Incarnation and the Church in a cosmic relation, the sociology saw human brotherhood as the corollary of both. Where the theology and the sociology were consciously held together, as in the Christian Social

[1] Ruth Kenyon, 'The Social Aspect of the Catholic Revival', in *Northern Catholicism*, p. 394.

Union, the name of Maurice was revered as a father and a founder.

IV

In the opening years of the new century the attitude of mind represented by *Lux Mundi* became dominant in Anglican theology. Its achievement was indeed impressive: for it held in one the faith of the Creeds and the ideas of evolution and immanence, the worship of the Prayer Book and a sensitive social conscience. And beyond the boundaries of this school, in circles less 'catholic' and more liberal, it became the sustained endeavour of theologians to create a synthesis of the Gospel and the prevailing philosophy and to find a Christo-centric view of the rationality of the universe. It is in terms of this endeavour that the theological work of William Temple has its vast importance.

There were, however, many pitfalls, and those who were engrossed in the task of synthesis were inclined to overlook them. In theology it was too often assumed that the Oxford idealism, derived from Hegel through T. H. Green or the Cairds, provided a theologian with a sort of normative set of presuppositions. The alliance of the Gospel and human reason was made to rest upon a too great confidence in the particular thought current at the time of the match-making, and it involved not a little blunting of these elements in the theology of the Bible which contradict an immanentist conception. Similarly in sociology it was too often assumed that the Logos doctrine sanctioned the Victorian ideas of progress

in a Christian guise; and Mr Reckitt has described
how even a mind as prophetic as Scott Holland's
could think of the 1914 war as an isolated interruption
of our civilization and not as the irruption of a disease
which lay deep within its life. Now, the reaction has
come. The catastrophes of our time have exposed the
weakness of this epoch of synthesis in theology and
have queried the hopes of its sociology. The climate
of thought has so changed that theologians commonly
see it as their function not to demonstrate the validity
of the Christian faith by the methods of contemporary
secular thought so much as to study the Biblical revelation in its own categories and to draw from it some
light to guide our steps in a dark world where diabolical forces are seeking whom they may devour.

The radical shifting of the theological perspective
has brought bewilderment both to the older and to the
younger theologians of our time. If the older sometimes fall into indiscriminate complaints of 'Barthian-
ism' in connection with studies and positions which
are new and unfamiliar to them, the younger sometimes use words like 'liberal' with habitual denigration
as if all that happened in the years between 1860 and
1920 was misleading and false. The change is movingly
described by Archbishop Temple in a letter quoted in
the last chapter of his biography. There is both tragedy
and greatness in the way in which Temple, after giving
his best years to the tasks of the older epoch, acknowledged its supersession by the newer. 'We must dig
the foundations deeper than in the pre-war years, or
in the inter-war years when we developed our pre-war

thoughts. And we must be content with less imposing structures. One day theology will take up again its larger and serener tasks and offer to a new Christendom its Christian map of life, its Christo-centric metaphysic. But that day will hardly dawn while any who are now already concerned with theology are still alive. The task that claims our labour now is far less alluring to one of my temperament and upbringing, yet there can be no doubt that in theology as in life we shall be rather enriched than impoverished, even though we are concerned to light beacons in the darkness rather than to illuminate the world, if we are more completely dominated in thought and aspiration by the redeeming acts of God in Jesus Christ.'[1]

It is possible that in the digging of the 'deeper foundations', of which Temple wrote, we may learn from one who said 'my business, because I am a theologian and have no vocation except for theology, is not to build but to dig.'[2] For the greatness of Maurice lies in the fact that, while his teaching paved the way for many of the achievements of theology and sociology in the late nineteenth and early twentieth centuries, it gave no sanction to those _naïvetés_ and false inferences of which we have just been thinking. He taught the doctrine of the Logos—but he was never an immanentist in the common meaning of the term. He taught that evolution might be seen as the continuous act of the Creator—but he never slipped into axioms about inevitable progress. He taught a Christian politics—

---

[1] F. A. Iremonger, _William Temple_, pp. 610-1.
[2] _Life of F.D.M._, II, p. 137.

but he never could identify this politics with the current assumptions about democracy. He pleaded for the light that lighteth every man, against theologies which virtually denied it—but he never lost sight of the uniqueness of the Word-made-flesh. And because the Bible which taught him these things taught him also that storm, famine, war and pestilence are the fate of civilizations which banish God, his message reaches beyond the liberal decades into the catastrophic times wherein we now find ourselves. The return to the living God of the Bible is a return to the constant theme of Maurice's writings. Yet these same writings sanction no lopsided transcendentalism, for they tell us of a divine foundation beneath our catastrophic world and of a divine image within our godless race. And while they tell of the vanity of every philosophy which leaves God out, they remind us that beneath heretical and godless ideologies there lie half-truths which are answered only when they have first been understood.

Far-reaching as were the conflicts of theology in which Maurice bore his part, it was within the Church of England that he bore it. The catholicity in which he believed was focused for him in the distinctive mission of the Church of England. He was Anglican to the core. Archbishop Fisher in his Cambridge sermon on reunion in 1946 declared that we who are Anglicans need to gain a firmer hold upon our own tradition. May it not be that we can learn from Maurice something of what our tradition really means? Derided by its exponents in his own day, Maurice shows us the roots of its unity. Things which we commonly grasp in one-sided antitheses, Maurice saw in their undivided oneness. But to learn from Maurice puts us in no danger of creating a Maurice-cult or of enrolling ourselves as Maurice's disciples. We are prevented from this, sometimes by the difficult idiom of his writing, always by his horror at gathering disciples around himself. And taking leave of him we shall turn, whither he directs us, to the 'Signs of the Constitution of the Catholic Church of Christ' and to the Father, the Son and the Holy Ghost.

BIBLIOGRAPHY

A complete bibliography of Maurice's writings is given at the beginning of the first volume of the Biography by his son, and a select one is given by Dr A. R. Vidler at the end of his Hale lectures. A list of articles upon Maurice in periodical literature is included in the bibliography in C. R. Sanders, *Coleridge and the Broad Church Movement*. The following list contains those books and articles which the present writer has found to be of special importance for the study of Maurice as a man and a theologian.

BETTANY, F. G. *Stewart Headlam: a Biography*, 1926.

CARLYLE, Thomas. *The Life of John Sterling*, 1851.

CHURCH, R. W. *Occasional Papers*, II, pp. 309-26, 1897.

COLLINS, W. E. 'F. D. Maurice', in *Typical English Churchmen from Parker to Maurice*, 1902.

GLOYN, C. K. *The Church in the Social Order, A Study of Anglican Social Theory from Coleridge to Maurice*, 1942.

HIGHAM, Florence. *Frederick Denison Maurice*, 1947.

HORT, A. F. *Life and Letters of F. J. A. Hort*, 1896.

HUTTON, R. H. *Essays, Theological and Literary*, I, 1877.

—— *Essays on some of the Modern Guides of English Thought in Matters of Faith*, 1887.

JENKINS, Claude. *F. D. Maurice and the New Reformation* (Maurice lectures for 1938), 1938.

MASTERMAN, C. F. G. *F. D. Maurice* (Leaders of the Church, 1800-1900), 1907.

MAURICE, Sir Frederick. *The Life of Frederick Denison Maurice, chiefly told in his own Letters*, 2 vols; fourth edn., 1885.

MOZLEY, J. B. *Essays Historical and Theological*, Vol. II, pp. 255-309, 3rd edn. 1892.

RAVEN, C. E. *Christian Socialism 1848-54*, 1920.

RECKITT, M. B. *Maurice to Temple* (the Scott Holland lectures for 1946), 1947.

RIGG, J. H. *Modern Anglican Theology* (Coleridge, Hare, Maurice, Kingsley and Jowett), 3rd edn., 1880.

SANDERS, C. R. *Coleridge and the Broad Church Movement*, 1942.

STEPHEN, Sir Leslie. 'F. D. Maurice' in *Dictionary of National Biography*, xxxvii, 1894.

—— 'Mr Maurice's Theology' in *Fortnightly Review*, xxi (1874), pp. 595-617.

VIDLER, A. R. *The Theology of F. D. Maurice* (Hale lectures for 1947), 1949.

WEDGWOOD, Julia. *Nineteenth Century Teachers* (includes studies of Coleridge, Maurice, and the Cambridge Apostles, reprinted from the *Contemporary Review* and other journals), 1909.

WOOD, H. G. *Frederick Denison Maurice*, 1950.

Amongst modern theologians who acknowledge their debt to Maurice mention should be made of Fr. Herbert Kelly, S.S.M., *The Gospel of God* (1928). 'I learnt almost everything first from Maurice; then I learnt it over again—several times'.

INDEX

ACLAND, SIR THOMAS, 98
Athanasian Creed, 56–7

BAILLIE, D. M., 54
Baptism, 26, 33–6
BEVAN, EDWYN, 54
Bible, 20, 23, 29, 70, 83–97, 113
Book of Common Prayer, 24, 39–40, 93
BREBANT, F. H., 54
Broad Church Party, 21, 32

CAMPBELL, MCLEOD, 69–70
CARLYLE, THOMAS, 9, 13, 19
Christian Socialism, 43–8, 100–101, 106–108
CHURCH, R. W., 18, 48, 106
COLENSO, G. W., 82–9
COLERIDGE, S. T., 13–20, 98
Creation, doctrine of, 22, 69–70, 91–2
CREED, J. M., 16–17, 105
Creeds, 14, 30, 56–7
CULLMANN, O., 54

DODD, C. H., 95

Episcopacy, 30–31
ERSKINE, T., 22
Eucharist, 30, 32
Evangelicals, 32

Fall of Man, 22, 71, 91
FISHER, ARCHBISHOP, 113

GLADSTONE, W. E., 30, 48
GORE, CHARLES, 108
GREEN, T. H., 108, 110
GRENSTED, L. W., 58, 61

HAMILTON, H. F., 37
HARE, JULIUS, 11–12, 28
HEADLAM, A. C., 58

HEADLAM, STEWART, 37, 106–8
Hegelianism, 110
HOLLAND, HENRY SCOTT, 37, 68
HORT, F. J. A., 15, 75, 102–3
HUGHES, TOM, 46
HUTTON, R. H., 72, 79, 89–90

KELLY, H. H., 116
KINGSLEY, CHARLES, 44–5, 100–1

LEE, J. P., 88
Liberalism, 32, 110–11
LIDDON, H. P., 106,
LIDGETT, J. SCOTT, 58
LUDLOW, J. M., 46–7
Lutheranism, 28
Lux Mundi, 108–9

MACMILLAN, DANIEL, 33
MANSEL, H. L., 72–80
MARCH, W. W. S., 72
MILL, J. S., 24–5, 75
MOZLEY, J. B., 41–2, 51–3

NEWMAN, J. H., 18, 30

Parties, 32–3
Platonism, 23, 49, 53–4, 70
PUSEY, E. B., 26–7, 86, 90

RAVEN, C. E., 46
RECKITT, M. B., 44, 111
Revelation, 15–21, 72–81
RIGG, J. H., 22, 23, 67

SANDERS, C. R., 15, 115
SHAFTESBURY, LORD, 90
SHAIRP, PRINCIPAL, 69–70
STEPHEN, LESLIE, 10
STERLING, JOHN, 11–14
STORR, V. F., 15
Subscription, 11

INDEX

TEMPLE, WILLIAM, 110–12
Tractarians, 18, 26–7, 34–7
Trinity, doctrine of, 10, 47, 54–5, 68
TULLOCH, J. H., 15, 37

WEDGWOOD, JULIA, 26, 41, 50, 78, 82
WESTCOTT, B. F., 17, 104
WILBERFORCE, S., 49

Printed in the United States
By Bookmasters